The Common Core Grammar Toolkit

Using Mentor Texts to Teach the Language Standards in Grades 9–12

Sean Ruday

Routledge
Taylor & Francis Group

NEW YORK AND LONDON

First published 2018
by Routledge
711 Third Avenue, New York, NY 10017

and by Routledge
2 Park Square, Milton Park, Abingdon, Oxon, OX14 4RN

Routledge is an imprint of the Taylor & Francis Group, an informa business

© 2018 Taylor & Francis

Library of Congress Cataloging-in-Publication Data
A catalog record for this book has been requested

ISBN: 978-1-138-30259-4 (hbk)
ISBN: 978-1-138-30260-0 (pbk)
ISBN: 978-1-315-17866-0 (ebk)

Typeset in Palatino and Formata
by Apex Covantage, LLC

Visit the eResources: www.routledge.com/9781138302600

The Common Core Grammar Toolkit

The Common Core's language standards can seem overwhelming—students need to learn specific, complex grammar rules at each grade level. *The Common Core Grammar Toolkit* to the rescue! In this comprehensive guide, author Sean Ruday shows how you can make grammar instruction fun and meaningful.

You will learn how to...

- ◆ Teach the Common Core's language standards for grades 9–12 by presenting each grammar rule as a useful writing tool.
- ◆ Use mentor texts—excerpts from great literature—to help students understand grammar in action.
- ◆ Promote metacognition along the way, so that students become responsible for their own learning.

The book thoroughly covers how to teach the Common Core's language standards for grades 9–12, on topics such as varying syntax for effect, using domain-specific words and phrases, analyzing nuances in word meanings, using semicolons to link related clauses, and more. You'll learn how to present each of these grammar rules to your students as tools that will help them improve their writing. You'll also find resources designed to provide you with extra support, including reproducible classroom-ready charts and forms, an annotated bibliography of suggested mentor texts for each grammar rule, and a guide for teachers and administrators interested in using the book for group-based professional development. With *The Common Core Grammar Toolkit*, you'll have a clear game plan for encouraging your students to use language more purposefully and effectively.

Sean Ruday is an associate professor of English Education at Longwood University and a former classroom teacher. He is also a Co-President of the Assembly for the Teaching of English Grammar. He frequently writes and presents on innovative ways to improve students' literacy learning.

Other Toolkit Books Available from Sean Ruday
(www.routledge.com/eyeoneducation)

The Common Core Grammar Toolkit:
Using Mentor Texts to Teach the Language Standards in Grades 6–8

The Common Core Grammar Toolkit:
Using Mentor Texts to Teach the Language Standards in Grades 3–5

The Multimedia Writing Toolkit:
Helping Students Incorporate Graphics and Videos for Authentic Purposes, Grades 3–8

The Argument Writing Toolkit:
Using Mentor Texts in Grades 6–8

The Informational Writing Toolkit:
Using Mentor Texts in Grades 3–5

The Narrative Writing Toolkit:
Using Mentor Texts in Grades 3–8

Contents

eResources

The appendices of this book can also be downloaded and printed for classroom use. You can access these downloads by visiting the book product page on our website: www.routledge.com/9781138302600. Then click on the tab that says "eResources," and select the files. They will begin downloading to your computer.

Meet the Author

Sean Ruday is an Associate Professor of English Education at Longwood University. He began his teaching career at a public school in Brooklyn, NY, and has taught English and language arts in New York, Massachusetts, and Virginia. Sean is a Co-President of the Assembly for the Teaching of English Grammar—a grammar-focused affiliate of the National Council of Teachers of English. He is the Founder and Editor of the *Journal of Literacy Innovation* and the editor of the *Virginia English Journal*. Some publications in which his articles have appeared are: *Journal of Teaching Writing, Journal of Language and Literacy Education, Contemporary Issues in Technology and Teacher Education,* and the *Yearbook of the Literacy Research Association*. His professional website is seanruday.weebly.com. You can follow him on Twitter @SeanRuday. This is his seventh book with Routledge Eye On Education.

Acknowledgements

I am thankful for all of the support I received while writing this book. I'd love to particularly acknowledge some individuals who helped make this project possible:

- The wonderful teachers who shared their thoughts with and gave me the opportunity to work with them and their students.
- The amazing students whose ideas, insights, and writings are included in this book.
- This book's editor, Lauren Davis, whose influence and support have been instrumental to my writing career.
- Wade Edwards, chair of Longwood University's Department of English and Modern Language, whose leadership and guidance I appreciate tremendously.
- My parents, Bob and Joyce Ruday, for all that they have done for me.
- My wife, Clare Ruday, who brightens my life by bringing humor and happiness to it.

What Should High School Grammar Instruction Look Like?

Smiling (and blushing a bit from the attention), I entered a school's auditorium to the sound of applause. People don't normally cheer my arrival, but this wasn't just any collection of individuals; a school district invited me to talk with its high school English teachers about strategies for teaching grammar in engaging and effective ways. After the warm reception, teachers and administrators began to share their concerns: "Sure, I know some ways to teach grammar," explained a teacher, "but I definitely don't know the *best* way. I can use textbooks and workbooks, but that doesn't get any kind of results with my ninth and tenth graders."

"Yeah," interjected another, "I need help with coming up with grammar activities that will actually help my students and not make them so bored that they either goof off or act like they'll fall asleep."

Several others in the room shared similar ideas: they knew, from their own experiences as well as professional reading they had done on the topic, that out-of-context grammar instruction like worksheets and textbook exercises doesn't help students become better writers and typically create boring English classes. They wanted new ideas for teaching grammar that would help their students understand and use grammatical concepts while also engaging them.

"I have a question for all of you," I told the teachers in the room. "Did you become a high school English teacher to discuss literature with your students?"

"Absolutely! I love talking about and studying literature," shared a teacher.

"Me, too," commented another. "I want to help students love literature as much I do."

"Same here," yet another teacher stated. "Reading great writers opened up a whole new world for me as a young person. I wanted to share that with the next generation."

"Wonderful," I responded. "Those are fantastic insights about the power of literature. Would it be accurate to say that the study of great literature is essential to your work as an English teacher?"

"Definitely!" exclaimed a teacher. "It's what I do best and what I spend the most time doing with my students."

A number of other teachers nodded in agreement, and I continued, "I'm thrilled to hear this because you and I are going to discuss how the study of outstanding literature can help students learn grammar. Sometimes people think of these two things as opposed; they feel that grammar and literature should be taught separately, but this just isn't the case. Grammatical concepts are tools that writers use to convey their ideas as effectively as possible. There's no need to resort to grammar workbooks and out-of-context exercises when you have so many excellent examples of published texts that can guide your grammar instruction."

This opening vignette captures issues in high school grammar instruction and the solution that this book provides to these issues. The Common Core State Standards (2010) and other rigorous, recently-revised state standards emphasize grammar instruction at all grade levels, leading to increased focus on grammar instruction in all grade levels—including high school, a time many teachers (such as those described in the opening vignette) associate primarily with literary analysis. With increased focus on grammar instruction in today's schools and standards, the natural response of many teachers and administrators is to move to out-of-context worksheets (Troia and Olinghouse, 2013), despite the fact that seminal research on this topic has long indicated that such instructional practices don't actually make students better writers (Kolln and Hancock, 2005; Weaver, 1998).

This book describes an instructional approach that integrates grammar instruction into the meaningful and analytical discussions of fiction and nonfiction that are essential to the work done in high school English classrooms. With this text as your guide, you'll no longer feel the need to give your students the stand-alone grammar worksheets and activities that experts on the topic advise against; instead, you'll be able to integrate grammar instruction into the great pieces of writing you already teach, streamlining your instructional practices and maximizing effectiveness!

In this introductory chapter, we'll explore the essential components of this book's approach to effective grammar instruction:

- The toolkit approach to teaching grammar.
- The importance of metacognition to understanding grammar.
- How effective grammar instruction leads to college- and career-readiness.
- What to expect in this book, including the specific Common Core Language Standards it addresses.

The Toolkit Approach to Teaching Grammar

The grammar instruction described in this book is based on the idea that grammatical concepts are tools that authors use to convey their ideas as effectively as possible. Just as craftspeople use particular tools to achieve certain results, the best authors use particular grammatical concepts to express information in specific ways. For example, just as a builder would use a saw in one situation and a hammer in another based on what she or he is trying to create, an author would use a participial phrase in one instance and an absolute phrase in a different situation based on the information he or she is trying to express.

An essential aspect of the toolkit approach to grammar instruction is the concept of a mentor text, an existing piece of writing used to show students a particular writing strategy (Fletcher and Portalupi, 2001). In this book, we'll explore many high-school level mentor texts from both fiction and nonfiction that convey effective uses of the grammatical concepts we'll explore. For example, in this excerpt from *The Great Gatsby* (Fitzgerald, 1925), author F. Scott Fitzgerald uses the participial phrase "flushed with his impassioned gibberish" as a tool to add detail and context to an independent clause: "Flushed with his impassioned gibberish he saw himself standing alone on the last barrier of civilization" (p. 137). This sentence, which describes the personality of antagonistic character Tom Buchanan, is an excellent mentor text for helping students understand this grammatical concept; it illustrates how authors can use participial phrases to craft in-depth descriptions of their characters.

Using mentor texts to help students understand grammatical concepts allows them to see the elements of grammar in authentic contexts, which facilitates their abilities to apply these concepts to their own written works (Robb, 2001). While out-of-context worksheets can make students good at completing those specific exercises, they don't provide many other benefits for students (Clark, 2010). In contrast, showing students published examples of texts that use certain grammatical concepts particularly well illustrates the importance of these concepts, provides concrete examples of their effective uses, and creates an organic way to bridge the gap between literature and grammar instruction.

The Importance of Metacognition to Understanding Grammar

Metacognition, the ability to reflect on one's cognitive process (Flavell, 1979), has long existed as a scientific phenomenon, but has recently been shown to enhance students' abilities to understand and use grammatical concepts (Ruday, 2013). In a metacognitive approach to grammar instruction, students analyze the grammatical choices authors make, reflect on how those choices impact the piece in which the concepts are used, and consider the grammatical concepts they decide to use in their own works.

For example, I recently conducted a discussion with a group of ninth graders that was designed to help them think carefully and analytically about the importance of subordinate clauses to effective writing. After introducing the basic components of the concept, I showed the students a sentence from Mark Twain's (1869) *The Innocents Abroad* that uses a humorous subordinate clause to provide context and detail to an associated independent clause: "If you wish to inflict a heartless and malignant punishment upon a young person, pledge him to keep a journal a year" (p. 42).

My students and I worked together to identify the subordinate clause, "If you wish to inflict a heartless and malignant punishment upon a young person," and then discussed its impact on the piece. "Why do you think this subordinate clause is important to the sentence?" I asked them.

To my delight, a number of students posed thoughtful responses about the clause's significance; one explained, "It shows what Twain thinks keeping a journal will do to somebody."

"And it makes the sentence make a lot more sense," added another, "because the sentence without [the subordinate clause] wouldn't say much. With [the subordinate clause], we can understand what Mark Twain is trying to say much better."

"Excellent insights!" I replied. "I really love how your responses focus on the significance of this subordinate clause to the information that the author is trying to convey. When you think about grammar, I don't want you to just think about identifying mistakes; I want you to think about why authors use certain grammatical concepts and what those concepts add to their writing." Students around the classroom nod and I continue: "This also applies to your own writing. When you apply a grammatical concept to your writing, you should do it purposefully, with a clear understanding of why you're using that concept. In our next class, we'll think about subordinate clauses in relation to writing by exploring how we can use them to enhance statements in the pieces we're writing in class."

While this conversation was specifically about subordinate clauses, it also addressed the larger idea of thinking analytically about the benefits and uses of all grammatical concepts. As I continued to work with these students—and all of the others described in this book—I helped them develop their metacognitive skills by giving them the framework needed to think carefully and critically about how and why authors use particular grammatical tools in their works. As you read this book, you'll learn the instructional strategies that help students think in metacognitive and analytical ways about grammatical concepts that enhance writing.

How Effective Grammar Instruction Leads to College- and Career-Readiness

A popular topic in education is the idea of college- and career-readiness, defined as the skills and strategies students need to succeed in a range of careers and courses of college study following their graduation from high school (Core Standards, 2010); this idea is central to the Common Core State Standards as well as other revised and rigorous state standards. While college- and career-readiness can take different forms across various subjects, the in-depth understanding of the uses and attributes of grammatical concepts is an important skill for high school students to develop as they prepare for their futures. This linguistic ability is widely recognized by employers; in a July 2016 article in *Entrepreneur* magazine, author and CEO

Bennat Berger asserts, "…professionals with the skills to communicate their ideas effectively go a long way in any workplace" (Berger, 2016).

Students who are able to think critically about and skillfully use grammatical concepts can communicate ideas in the way Berger describes. For example, students who understand the benefits and functions of relative clauses in effective writing can use them in all forms of communication. This in-depth understanding begins with students thinking about how and why published authors use these concepts, transitions to students using the concepts in their own works, and culminates in them reflecting on the concepts' significance to the pieces they created.

To illustrate this idea, let's look at a sentence from Charles Dickens' (1861) novel *Great Expectations* that contains a relative clause and consider its relation to students' future communication: "An elderly woman, whom I had seen before as one of the servants who lived in the supplementary house across the back court-yard, opened the gate" (p. 397). Without the relative clause, "whom I had seen before as one of the servants who lived in the supplementary house across the back court-yard," this sentence would be much less detailed, reading "An elderly woman opened the gate." While not all of our students will be writing fiction after high school, they can all benefit from learning to use information-adding relative clauses like the one in this sentence. In academic papers, professional writing, and everyday office-oriented correspondence, the ability to add important identifying and descriptive information using grammatical concepts such as relative clauses can help enhance our students' chances of future success. We teachers can help students understand the utility of these grammar tools by showing them how they can apply the tools to many written genres; they can use these strategies in pieces they compose for any subject area or for pieces they create on their own. For example, in this book, we'll meet a student writer who uses relative and subordinate clauses to make his description of success strategies for the video game *Madden 17* as effective as possible.

What to Expect in This Book

This book provides thoughtful, research-based solutions for high school English teachers looking to teach grammar in the context of great literature. (In this book, the term "literature" refers to works of fiction, drama, and literary nonfiction to reflect the various forms of writing examined in the literary analysis that takes place in high school classrooms.) It describes specific, classroom-ready practices teachers can use to help their students reach in-depth understandings of important grammatical concepts and is divided into four sections:

◆ Section one, which addresses grammatical concepts aligned with the Common Core Language Standards for grades nine and ten: the use of key phrases to convey specific meanings and add variety to writing, the use of key clauses for this same purpose, the use of semicolons to link closely related independent clauses, and strategies for interpreting and understanding figurative language.

◆ Section two, which explores grammatical concepts aligned with the Common Core Language Standards for grades eleven and twelve: the variation of syntax for effect, strategies for analyzing nuances in the meanings of words with similar denotations, and the use of domain-specific words and phrases such as strong verbs and specific nouns.

Figure 00.1 lists the grammatical concepts addressed in sections one and two, the chapter in which each one is discussed, and the Common Core Language Standard associated with each chapter.

Figure 00.1 Grammatical Concepts, Chapters, and Standards

Grammatical Concept	Discussed in Chapter	Related Common Core Language Standard
Purposefully Use Key Phrases to Convey Specific Meanings and Add Variety	Chapter One	L.9–10.1.B
Purposefully Use Key Clauses to Convey Specific Meanings and Add Variety	Chapter Two	L.9–10.1.B
Use Semicolons to Link Closely Related Independent Clauses	Chapter Three	L.9–10.2.A
Interpret Figures of Speech and Understand Their Roles in a Text	Chapter Four	L.9–10.5.A
Vary Syntax for Effect	Chapter Five	L.11–12.3.A
Analyze Nuances in the Meanings of Words with Similar Denotations	Chapter Six	L.11–12.5.B
Use Domain-Specific Words and Phrases	Chapter Seven	L.11–12.6

◆ To make this book as useful as possible, I've organized each chapter in sections one and two into the following sections:

◆ "What Is It?" This section provides an overview of the grammatical concept addressed in the chapter, ensuring readers understand the fundamental components of the concept before continuing on in the chapter.

◆ "Why Is It Important to Good Writing?" This section explores why the grammatical concept discussed in the chapter is an important tool for effective writing, examining its impact on published works in which it appears and describing the benefits associated with its use.

- ◆ "A Classroom Snapshot." Each classroom snapshot describes one of my experiences teaching students in high school English classes about the grammatical concepts described in this book and why those concepts are important tools for effective writing. These snapshots are included so that you can see how I taught my students to think analytically and metacognitively about grammatical concepts and learn from these examples as you work with your own students.
- ◆ "Instructional Recommendations." All of the chapters in sections one and two close with specific instructional recommendations for you to keep in mind when helping your students understand specific grammatical tools and apply those tools to their own works.
- ◆ Section three, which focuses on "Putting It Together." One chapter in this section features activities and rubrics to use when assessing your students' understandings of the grammatical concepts described in this book, while the second chapter in the section provides final thoughts and tips that will help you put the ideas discussed in this book into action in your own classroom.
- ◆ Section four, which contains useful resources that will provide you with extra support as you teach your students about the grammatical tools described in this text:
  - ◆ The book's reference list.
  - ◆ Appendix A, an annotated bibliography, which lists the works of literature featured in the book, a key grammatical concept found in each work, and the Common Core Language Standard associated with that concept.
  - ◆ Appendix B, featuring reproducible charts and forms you can use in your classroom.
  - ◆ Appendix C, containing a guide for teachers and administrators interested in using this book for a professional book study.

Reshaping one's grammar instruction so that it moves away from worksheets and exercises and toward analytic, literature-based discussions of grammatical tools that authors use in purposeful ways is no easy task, but this book will provide you with the ideas, strategies, and texts that will allow you to make this important shift in your classroom. As we explore the book's chapters, we'll look with new eyes at excerpts from great literature, considering how the authors of those works use grammatical concepts with clear understandings of their benefits and how we can help our high school students do similar work in their own writing. If you're ready to begin this exploration, keep reading!

Section 1

Grammatical Concepts Aligned with Common Core Language Standards for Grades 9 and 10

1

Purposefully Use Key Phrases to Convey Specific Meanings and Add Variety

Let's begin our discussion of effective grammar instruction by exploring what means to use selected phrases to convey intended meanings and add variety while writing. First, we'll examine what this grammatical tool can look like in practice and then consider how it can enhance a piece of writing. Next, we'll look at a description of a lesson on this topic and then conclude by examining some recommendations to keep in mind when helping your students understand this grammatical concept.

What Is It?

An effective way for authors to maximize the effectiveness of a piece of writing is to use phrases that help them develop the ideas in their works. The Common Core State Standards support the use of this grammatical tool; Standard L.9–10.1 calls for students to "use various types of phrases … to convey specific meanings and add variety and interest to writing or presentations" (Core Standards, 2010). While there are a number of kinds of phrases that can be used for these purposes, in this chapter we'll take an in-depth look at three widely-used kinds of phrases that can significantly impact a piece of writing: prepositional, participial, and absolute phrases. These three types of phrases are specifically mentioned in Standard L.9–10.1 as being important concepts for students to understand. Let's take a look at the features of each of these phrase types.

Prepositional Phrases

Prepositional phrases begin with prepositions and end with nouns or pronouns that serve as objects of those prepositions. For example, in the prepositional phrase "across the field" "across" is a preposition and "field" is the object of that preposition. In the context of a full sentence, this prepositional phrase could read, "Antonio caught the ball and sprinted across the field." An interesting feature of prepositional phrases is that they can be adjectival or adverbial depending on how they're used and the kind of information they provide. The prepositional phrase in the sentence "Antonio caught the ball and sprinted across the field" is adverbial because it describes where Antonio sprinted. Conversely, the prepositional phrase "in the locker room" in the sentence "The players in the locker room are excited" is adjectival because it provides descriptive information about the noun "players." Figure 1.1 provides key information about prepositional phrases.

Participial Phrases

Participial phrases begin with present or past participles and provide descriptive information about nouns in a piece of writing. The present participle is called the "-ing" form of a verb and the past participle is the "-en" form of a verb. The past participle of a regular verb is formed by adding "-ed" to the end of the verb. (However, past participles of irregular verbs vary and are often not governed by specific rules or patterns.) In the sentence "Waving to the crowd, the players entered the stadium," "waving to the crowd" is a participial phrase that begins with a present participle. By contrast, the sentence "Buried by pirates, the treasure remained undiscovered for centuries" uses a participial phrase—"buried by pirates"—that contains a past participle. Note that each of these participial phrases describes nouns in their respective sentences: "waving to the crowd" provides information about "the players", while "buried by pirates" modifies "pirates." Figure 1.2 illustrates important details about participial phrases.

Figure 1.1 Important Details about Prepositional Phrases

Grammatical Concept	Prepositional Phrase
What is a prepositional phrase?	A prepositional phrase is a group of words that begins with a preposition and end with a noun or pronoun that serves as an object of the preposition. Prepositional phrases can be adjectival or adverbial depending on how they're used and the kind of information they provide.
What are some examples?	"across the field" "in the locker room"
What do they look like in sentences?	"Antonio caught the ball and sprinted across the field." "The players in the locker room are excited."

Figure 1.2 Important Details about Participial Phrases

Grammatical Concept	Participial Phrase
What is a participial phrase?	A participial phrase begins with either a present or past participle and is used to provide descriptive information about a noun in a sentence.
What are some examples?	Participial phrase with present participle: "Waving to the crowd." Participial phrase with past participle: "Buried by pirates."
What do they look like in sentences?	"Waving to the crowd, the players entered the stadium." "Buried by pirates, the treasure remained undiscovered for centuries."

Absolute Phrases

While prepositional phrases add either adjectival or adverbial information, depending on their usage, and participial phrases provide readers with adjectival information, absolute phrases play a different role: they introduce information "related to the sentence as a whole, not to any one of its parts" (Kolln and Funk, 2012, p. 199). In other words, absolute phrases don't describe a specific noun or verb in a sentence: they provide context and detail related to the sentence in its entirety, making them full-sentence modifiers (Kolln and Funk, 2012). An absolute phrase contains a noun or noun phrase and a post-noun modifier, such as a participle, participial phrase, prepositional phrase, or other word or phrase that describes the noun. For example, the absolute phrase "his hands in his pockets" begins with a noun phrase ("his hands"), which is then followed by modifying information (in this case, the prepositional phrase "in his pockets"). This absolute phrase could appear in the sentence "Jeff walked around campus on a cold winter morning, his hands in his pockets." Note how this absolute phrase provides information about the context of the sentence as a whole, making it a full-sentence modifier rather than an adjectival or adverbial. Figure 1.3 provides key information about absolute phrases.

Why Is This Concept Important to Effective Writing?

The purposeful use of phrases aligns with the toolkit approach at the heart of this book: each type of phrase is a tool an author would use with a particular purpose in mind. Prepositional, participial, and absolute phrases are all effective ways to add detail and variety to a piece of writing, but

Figure 1.3 Important Details about Absolute Phrases

Grammatical Concept	Absolute Phrase
What is an absolute phrase?	An absolute phrase is a full-sentence modifier that conveys information "related to the sentence as a whole, not to any one of its parts" (Kolln and Funk, 2012, p. 199). An absolute phrase contains a noun or noun phrase and a post-noun modifier, such as a participle, participial phrase, prepositional phrase, or other word or phrase that describes the noun.
What are some examples?	"his hands in his pockets." "crowd noise ringing in his ears."
What do they look like in sentences?	"Jeff walked around campus on a cold winter morning, his hands in his pockets." "Crowd noise ringing in his ears, the coach called a timeout."

each type can benefit a written work in a unique way that aligns directly with its attributes and features. Given the individualized nature of these three phrases, we'll take a look at the impact of each one individually, examining and unpacking examples from these concepts from literature.

Why Are Prepositional Phrases Important to Effective Writing?

Prepositional phrases are great tools for adding descriptive details to a piece, such as the time or place of an event and where a person or object is located. In his 1946 book *Animal Farm*, George Orwell uses a variety of prepositional phrases to help readers understand important information. For example, when Boxer, the farm's hardworking horse, is injured, Orwell uses purposefully-selected prepositional phrases to convey details of his attempted recovery. The sentence "For the next two days Boxer remained in his stall" (p. 82) uses the prepositional phrases "for the next two days" and "in his stall" to illustrate where Boxer tried to recover and how long he was there. Just a few pages later in the text, Orwell again utilizes a number of prepositional phrases, stating, "No one stirred in the farmhouse before noon on the following day…" (p. 86). Without the prepositional phrases "in the farmhouse," "before noon," and "on the following day," the reader would only learn that "no one stirred." The prepositional phrases Orwell uses in these examples are crucial to readers' in-depth understandings of *Animal Farm*.

Why Are Participial Phrases Important to Effective Writing?

Participial phrases are tools authors can use to effectively and clearly describe the attributes of the nouns in their works; a well-used participial phrase helps readers understand details about a noun's characteristics, features, or background. For example, in *Wuthering Heights,* Emily Brontë (1847) uses the participial phrase "dripping with snow and water" to clearly describe a character's hair, allowing readers to visualize the individual's appearance: "The intruder was Mrs. Heathcliff—she certainly seemed in no laughing predicament: her hair streamed on her shoulders, dripping with snow and water…" (p. 172). While this sentence would still be grammatically correct without the participial phrase, its omission would take away the detail that helps readers imagine this scene. At another point in *Wuthering Heights,* Brontë uses the participial phrase "edged with black" for a similar purpose; in the sentence "A letter, edged with black, announced the day of my master's return" (p. 199), the participial phrase adds descriptive information that makes the letter easier for readers to picture. These two participial phrases in *Wuthering Heights* enhance readers' experiences by providing key details about the nouns they describe.

Why Are Absolute Phrases Important to Effective Writing?

Absolute phrases are innovative and useful writing tools: they allow authors to focus readers' attentions on specific aspects of sentences. For example, in the previously-mentioned sentence "Jeff walked around campus on a cold winter morning, his hands in his pockets," the absolute phrase "his hands in his pockets" focuses our attention on that image. When explaining the impact of absolute phrases to students, I compare their use with how a photographer would employ a zoom lens: while sometimes a photographer might capture an image at a distance, there are other times when she would want a shot that zooms in more closely on a particular aspect of the image. Absolute phrases can provide this same "zoomed-in" effect: a sentence without an absolute phrase creates a more general feel, while a sentence containing an absolute phrase "zooms in" on a specific element of the sentence, inviting readers to focus primarily on that component. In the book *Fallen Angels*, author Walter Dean Myers (1988) uses the absolute phrase "wheels squealing" to direct readers' attentions to a particular aspect of a sentence: "Suddenly it picked up speed, wheels squealing, lurching from one side of the narrow street to the other" (p. 87). This sentence, which describes a car approaching a neighborhood, benefits from its absolute phrase: the phrase zooms in on the car's squealing wheels, allowing readers to clearly understand this component of the action. Absolute phrases like the ones described in this section allow authors to highlight especially important information, helping them take general sentences and turn them into more specific and detailed versions.

Now that we've explored the impact that purposefully selected phrases can have on a piece of writing, let's take a look inside a ninth-grade

English classroom and examine how my students worked to understand the importance of this concept.

A Classroom Snapshot

Early Monday morning is not a time I typically associate with enthusiastic ninth graders, but my students have pleasantly surprised me; right before the opening school bell rings, several students in my ninth-grade English class approach me to share how much they've been enjoying our recent grammar work: "This is so much more interesting than what we've ever done with grammar before," one shares. "I think looking at grammar in literature and talking about it is so much better than doing worksheets like we've done." Thrilled by this positive and insightful feedback, I reply, "I'm so happy to hear that! If you like what we've been doing with looking at and analyzing grammar in literature, you're going to love what we do today!"

For the past two classes, these students and I have been discussing the importance of purposefully using phrases to enhance the effectiveness of writing, exploring how well-used phrases can convey specific information and add variety to a piece. In our first meeting on the topic, we discussed the attributes of prepositional, participial, and absolute phrases and looked together at examples of those concepts in literature. Next, in our second meeting, we considered how the sentences containing those phrases would be different if the concept was not used. (For example, after we examined the previously described sentences from *Animal Farm* that contain prepositional phrases, we talked about what information we wouldn't know if George Orwell hadn't used those phrases.) In today's class, we'll build off of our previous work with an interactive small-group activity that calls for students to find an example of a prepositional, participial, or absolute phrase in a piece of literature and comment on its importance to the piece in which it was originally used.

The class period begins and I introduce the day's activity to the class: "Today, we're going to take the next step in our work on prepositional, participial, and absolute phrases. Instead of me showing you published examples of these concepts, you all are going to work in groups to find an example from literature of one of these phrases and analyze the impact it has on the text where you found it." I give each group of students a chart that they'll use to complete the activity; this chart, depicted in Figure 1.4, asks students to identify the title and author of the book they used for the activity, state a type of phrase they noticed in the text, note an excerpt from the text that contains that phrase, and finally analyze why that phrase is important to the sentence in which the author uses it. (A reproducible version of this chart is available in Appendix B.)

"Before you get started," I tell the students, "let's work together on the kind of identification and analysis you'll do for this activity." I put a copy of this chart on the document camera and explain, "For this example, I'm

Figure 1.4 Phrase Analysis Chart

Book Title and Author	Type of Phrase You Noticed	Excerpt that Contains Phrase	Why the Phrase is Important to the Text

going to use one of my favorite sentences from all of literature: 'The mass of men lead lives of quiet desperation' from Henry David Thoreau's *Walden* (Thoreau, 1854, p. 7). This sentence contains the prepositional phrase 'of quiet desperation.' To fill out this chart, I'll write the book title and author—*Walden* by Henry David Thoreau—in the first column. Next, in the second column, I'll write 'prepositional phrase' because that's the type of phrase I noticed in this sentence. After that, in the third column, I'll write the whole sentence. Finally, in the fourth column, I'll comment on why I think this prepositional phrase is important that what Thoreau is trying to say. In that column, I'm going to write, 'This prepositional phrase is important to the text because it explains the kind of lives that Thoreau believes most people lead. Without it, we wouldn't know this important information.'"

A number of students nod to indicate their understanding, and I continue: "So, that's an example of the analysis activity you'll do with your group members. You'll want to select a book from our classroom library and look for examples of the phrase types we've discussed. Once you find an example, you can use it, as well as the sentence in which it appears, to complete the analysis chart. I'll come around and check in with you while you work."

After about ten minutes have passed for the students to select texts, comb through them, identify key clauses, and analyze their importance, I sit down with the groups and ask them what they've found. I first meet with a group using Saul Bellow's (1958) novel *Henderson the Rain King*.

"How's it going?" I begin by asking the students.

"It's going really well!" exclaims a young lady in the group. "I love this book, and we found a good participial phrase."

"Fantastic!" I reply. "Tell me what you found."

"We found this excerpt here," replies another student in the group, "'…sitting above the clouds, I felt like an airborne seed' (p. 42). The participial phrase we found was 'sitting above the clouds.'"

"Great job!" I praise the students' work. "Why do you all think that participial phrase is important to the text?"

"We talked about how it's important because it describes what Henderson was doing when he felt like an airborne seed," responds one student.

"Yeah," adds another. "The participial phrase gives a lot more information to the reader and explains things a lot better than if it wasn't there. Without the phrase, [this excerpt] would be 'I felt like an airborne seed.' It wouldn't have much explanation. With it, we have a lot more explanation because we know more about what made Henderson feel this way."

"That's wonderful!" I exclaim. "I love how you discussed the impact of the participial phrase on the sentence! I was particularly impressed with the way you compared the sentence with the participial phrase with how it would look if the phrase wasn't used. Very nice job!"

Next, I pull up a chair alongside a group of students using Michael Crichton's (1990) novel *Jurassic Park*. "Great choice!" I say, pointing to the book. "What did you all notice about it?"

"We actually found a bunch of phrases," explains one student in the group, "but the one we picked out to use [for this activity] is an absolute phrase."

"Awesome," I reply. "Those can have a huge impact on a piece of writing. What did you find?"

"We found the absolute phrase 'his cheek pressed against the car door handle' in the sentence 'Tim Murphy lay in the Land Cruiser, his cheek pressed against the car door handle'" (p. 204), answers a student.

"Good job of identifying that example," I tell the group. "Absolute phrases can sometimes be hard to pick out, but you did that perfectly. Now, let's think about the final column on the chart: why do you think this absolute phrase is important?"

"I remember how you said in our last class that absolute phrases, like, zoom in on something in a sentence," states a group member, "and this absolute phrase totally does that. It zooms in on the description of [Tim Murphy] by focusing on his cheek and how it's pressed against the car handle."

"That's such a great response!" I call out. "I really love how you made a connection to our recent discussion about the way absolute phrases zoom in on a particular aspect of a sentence. I also love how you described the specific way this absolute phrase in *Jurassic Park* zooms in."

I check in with the other three groups of students and am similarly impressed with the phrases they've found and the analyses they've conducted. Closing up the class period, I commend their works: "I'm so proud of how well you all did on this activity today! Each group did a great job of finding a prepositional, participial, or absolute phrase in literature and thinking carefully about the importance of that phrase. Great job!"

Instructional Recommendations

In this section, I describe a step-by-step instructional process to use when teaching students about the purposeful uses of prepositional, participial, and absolute phrases. The instructional steps I recommend are: 1) Present students with published examples of these phrases and discuss the phrases' impacts; 2) Show students published sentences with the phrases removed and discuss the differences; 3) Ask students to work together to analyze the importance of these phrases; 4) Have students apply these phrases to their own writings; and 5) Help students reflect on the impacts these phrases have on the pieces they create. Since these steps are designed to help students apply their understandings of prepositional, participial, and absolute phrases, I suggest using the information at the beginning of this chapter (such as the charts in Figures 1.1, 1.2, and 1.3) to ensure that students understand the fundamental features of these phrases before beginning this instructional process.

1. Present students with published examples of these phrases and discuss the phrases' impacts.

I recommend beginning this instructional process by showing your students published examples of prepositional, participial, and absolute phrases and talking with them about the impacts those phrases have on the sentences in which they appear. When I recently did this with ninth graders, I began by sharing the excerpts from *Animal Farm, Wuthering Heights,* and *Fallen Angels* described in this chapter and highlighting examples of the focal phrases we were discussing. Next, I thought aloud about the information each phrase adds to the sentence in which it appears; doing so gave the students insights into how each phrase contributes to the effectiveness of the text, helping them understand that these grammatical concepts—as well as all others—are tools that authors use purposefully. For example, in a recent conversation on participial phrases, I projected the two previously mentioned examples of this concept from *Wuthering Heights* to the front of the room and explained how I felt each participial phrase enhances the text, noting specific information each phrase provided.

When I show students published examples of grammatical concepts, I often compare the experience with seeing animals in their natural habitats: "I'm showing you these published examples of prepositional, participial, and absolute phrases," I recently told the ninth graders with whom I was working, "because this is the best way to help you see how they're really used and the impact they can have. If you watch an animal in the zoo, you probably wouldn't learn as much about it as if you saw footage of it in nature. Looking at these published examples is like seeing grammar 'in nature.'" The experience of seeing published examples of grammatical concepts helps students begin to comprehend the importance of grammatical tools to effective writing. Once you feel like your students have developed solid foundational understandings of what prepositional, participial, and absolute phrases are and how they can impact a piece of writing, you can move to the next stage of this process.

2. Show students published sentences with the phrases removed and discuss the differences.

This instructional step places increased ownership and responsibility on the students by further involving them in interactive grammatical activities. To begin, I recommend showing students versions of the sentences you showed them in step one, revised to no longer contain the original prepositional, participial, or absolute phrase. When I share these revised examples, I like to juxtapose them next to the original versions, as this provides students with a visual representation of the distinctions between the two sentences and facilitates discussion of the differences.

For example, when talking with my students about prepositional phrases, I first displayed the sentence "For the next two days Boxer remained in his stall" from *Animal Farm* alongside a new version of the sentence without any prepositional phrases that read "Boxer remained." Next, I asked the students to talk with their small group members about how the sentences were different and to share some highlights from those conversations with the rest of the class. One group explained, "The second one is so basic that it just doesn't really make any sense. You really need those prepositional phrases to understand what's going on." Another group added, "The prepositional phrases contain things we need to know to get what the author's trying to tell us, like where Boxer was and how long he was there." After this discussion, I engaged the students in similar conversations about participial and absolute phrases, pairing published examples with revised versions that no longer contain the phrases and asking them to comment on the importance of the phrases to the original text. Once I'm satisfied with my students' awareness of these phrases and understandings of their importance, I'll move to the third step of this instructional process.

3. Ask students to work together to analyze the importance of these phrases.

At this point, I recommend releasing even more responsibility to students by asking them to work in groups to identify and analyze the importance of prepositional, participial, or absolute phrases in published texts. To maximize students' chances of success on this activity, I suggest giving them a copy of the chart depicted in Figure 1.4 (found earlier in this chapter) to guide their identification and analysis of effectively used phrases in published texts. In addition, before students work together on this activity, I like to model an example for them; this allows them to hear me think aloud as I identify and analyze key phrases in a piece. For example, in this chapter's classroom snapshot, I describe my experience modeling the activity by identifying and analyzing the prepositional phrase "of quiet desperation" found in Henry David Thoreau's *Walden*. Demonstrating this process for students clarifies the expectations of the activity before they begin working on it.

Once the students are in groups and ready to work on the activity, I ask them to look through published texts to identify prepositional, participial, or absolute phrases to use for the activity. After each group has taken a few minutes to get started on their identifications and analyses, I like to sit down with each group and ask the students in it to tell me what they're noticing. This is a great opportunity to see how well students are grasping the topic and answer any questions they have. While most students at this point in the process have good understandings of prepositional, participial, and absolute phrases and their potential impact on a piece of writing, you may encounter some groups who misidentify a phrase or are unsure of why the phrase they find is important to the text. These discussions with small groups of students are excellent times to address and clarify any misunderstandings before continuing the instructional process.

4.   Have students apply these phrases to their own writings.

Now that students have examined, identified, and analyzed prepositional, participial, and absolute phrases, I recommend asking them to apply these phrases to their own works. When I do this with my students, I encourage them to focus on applying one strategy at a time to their writings. For example, when talking with my ninth graders about revising their memoirs, I first worked with them on adding prepositional phrases to enhance details about time and place in their works. Next, the students and I focused on them including participial phrases in their pieces to provide important descriptive information. Finally, the students and I concentrated on how they could incorporate absolute phrases to direct readers' attention to important aspects of situations.

I like to have students apply these phrases at both the drafting and revision stages of their works. At the drafting stage, students purposefully incorporate prepositional, participial, or absolute phrases into the initial drafts of their pieces, using them to provide important details and information to readers. When students apply these concepts at the revision stage, they examine their existing pieces, looking for sections that could be enhanced by one of these phrase types. I recently worked with a student who added absolute phrases while revising the memoir he was writing, using them to zoom in on important details. The excerpt from this student's work depicted in Figure 1.5 uses the absolute phrases "teeth clenched" and "our foreheads covered in sweat" to describe his experience canoeing.

5. Help students reflect on the impacts these phrases have on the pieces they create.

I recommend concluding this instructional process by asking students to reflect on how the phrases they incorporated impacted their works. To facilitate these reflections, I ask my students three questions that call for them to consider which kinds of phrases they added and how those phrases affected their writings: 1) What type or types of phrases did you incorporate into your writing?; 2) How do you feel those phrases impacted the piece you created?; and 3) How do you think your piece would be different if you did not use those phrases? By responding to these questions, students can enhance their metacognitive awareness of how purposefully selected prepositional, participial, and absolute phrases can influence their writings.

The student who created the memoir about canoeing described in the previous recommendation commented on the impact of the absolute phrases he used by saying, "The absolute phrases I used, 'our foreheads covered in sweat' and 'teeth clenched', made my memoir better by telling readers about important parts of the events I was describing. When I said, 'Teeth clenched, we rowed with all of our might to get across the finish line first,' the absolute phrase 'teeth clenched' gives readers important description and information to let them know what was going on." This student continued to explain, "If I didn't use [absolute phrases], I would be able to give the readers the full description. Like, they'd still know about the canoeing, but they wouldn't know the extra details the absolute phrases add, like our foreheads being covered in sweat and our teeth being clenched."

Figure 1.5 Student Memoir Excerpt, Featuring Absolute Phrases

" We're almost there!" my counselor called.

"I can see the finish!" My group was close to winning the all-camp challenge, but first we had to guide our canoe the final 100 yards down the last stretch of river before any other groups did.

"We can do it!" my friend Josh and I screamed together, our foreheads covered in sweat. We didn't care how hot it was or how much we were sweating, we needed to win! Teeth clenched, we rowed with all of our might to get across the finish line first.

Final Thoughts on Purposefully Using Key Phrases to Convey Specific Meanings and Add Variety

- The purposeful use of key phrases to enhance the quality of a piece of writing is included in Common Core Language Standard L.9–10.1.
- Three phrases that can especially improve a work are prepositional phrases, participial phrases, and absolute phrases.
    - Prepositional phrases begin with a preposition and end with an object of a preposition.
    - Participial phrases can begin with either a present or past participle.
    - Absolute phrases begin with a noun or noun phrase, which is followed by a post-noun modifier, such as a participle, participial phrase, prepositional phrase, or other word or phrase that describes the noun.
- Each of these three kinds of phrases enhances a piece of writing in a way that is unique to its characteristics.
    - Prepositional phrases are great tools for adding descriptive details to a piece, such as the time or place of an event and where a person or object is located.
    - Participial phrases are tools authors can use to effectively and clearly describe the attributes of the nouns in their works.
    - Absolute phrases are innovative and useful writing tools that allow authors to focus readers' attentions on specific aspects of sentences.
- When teaching students about the purposeful use of prepositional, participial, and absolute phrases:
    - Present students with published examples of these phrases and discuss the phrases' impacts.
    - Show students published sentences with the phrases removed and discuss the differences.
    - Ask students to work together to analyze the importance of these phrases.
    - Have students apply these phrases to their own writings.
    - Help students reflect on the impacts these phrases have on the pieces they create.

2

Purposefully Use Key Clauses to Convey Specific Meanings and Add Variety

In this chapter, we'll explore another way authors convey specific meanings and add variety while writing: through the implementation of purposefully and carefully used clauses. First, we'll look at two particularly effective kinds of clauses and examine how those clauses can impact a piece of writing. Then we'll check out a description of a lesson on this grammatical concept. Finally, we'll consider some key recommendations to keep in mind when teaching your students about the purposeful use of clauses in writing.

What Is It?

A clause is defined as "a structure with subject and a predicate" (Kolln and Funk, 2012, p. 351). However, despite this straightforward definition, the clause is a complex grammatical concept because of the many forms it can take. Not only can clauses be independent or dependent (an independent clause can function on its own as a sentence, while a dependent clause cannot), but dependent clauses can also be further divided into specific types, such as nominal, relative, and subordinate. Common Core Standard L.9–10.1 calls for students to "use various types" of clauses "to convey specific meanings and add variety and interest to writing or presentations." Two especially significant types of clauses that can make an impact on a piece of writing are relative and subordinate clauses; we'll examine each of these in this chapter.

Relative Clauses

Relative clauses are dependent clauses that are used to describe nouns in sentences. These clauses either begin with relative pronouns (*who, whose, whom, which,* and *that*) or with relative adverbs (*where, when,* and *why*).

For example, the sentence "Mr. Smith, who played in the National Football League, is our school's new football coach" contains the relative clause "who played in the National Football League" (which begins with the relative pronoun "who"). Another relative clause can be found in the sentence "I'm excited for Friday night, when our team will play its first game"; in this example, the relative clause "when our team will play its first game" begins with the relative adverb "when." Figure 2.1 highlights key information about relative clauses.

Subordinate Clauses

Subordinate clauses are dependent clauses that begin with subordinating conjunctions and provide additional context and detail about the information conveyed in an associated independent clause. Some subordinating conjunctions that are used especially frequently are *if, since, although, because,* and *until.* Unlike relative clauses, which are used to describe nouns, subordinate clauses explain the relationships between ideas in sentences, such as in the example, "Since she is running in today's race, Jane is wearing her lucky sneakers." This sentence uses the subordinate clause "since she is running in today's race" to explain why Jane is wearing her lucky sneakers. (Note that the subordinate clause begins with the subordinating conjunction "since.") Kolln and Funk (2012) explain that many subordinate clauses function as "full-sentence modifiers" because they are used to "modify the idea of the whole sentence" (p. 195). Figure 2.2 addresses important information about subordinate clauses.

Figure 2.1 Important Details about Relative Clauses

Grammatical Concept	Relative Clause
What is a relative clause?	A relative clause is a dependent clause used to describe a noun in a sentence. These clauses can begin with either relative pronouns (*who, whose, whom, which,* and *that*) or relative adverbs (*where, when,* and *why*).
What are some examples?	"who played in the National Football League" (this example begins with the relative pronoun *who*) "when our team will play its first game" (this example begins with the relative adverb *when*)
What do they look like in sentences?	"Mr. Smith, who played in the National Football League, is our school's new football coach." "I'm excited for Friday night, when our team will play its first game."

Figure 2.2 Important Details about Subordinate Clauses

Grammatical Concept	Subordinate Clause
What is a relative clause?	A subordinate clause is a dependent clause that begins with a subordinating conjunction (such as *if, since, although, because,* and *until*) and provides additional context and detail about the information in an independent clause.
What are some examples?	"since she is running in today's race" "although it was her first marathon"
What do they look like in sentences?	"Since she is running in today's race, Jane is wearing her lucky sneakers." "Although it was her first marathon, Kate finished ahead of many experienced runners."

Why Is This Concept Important to Effective Writing?

Like the purposeful use of different types of phrases described in Chapter 1, the strategic use of relative and subordinate clauses aligns with this book's central argument that grammatical concepts are most effective when they are used with clear understandings of the benefits associated with them. In this section, we'll explore in detail the importance of relative and subordinate clauses to effective writing, examining published versions of these concepts and discussing their impact on the works in which they appear.

Why Are Relative Clauses Important to Effective Writing?

Relative clauses are important to effective writing because they can provide adjectival information that allows readers to reach more developed understandings of people, places, things, and ideas in a text. In his 1962 novel *Something Wicked This Way Comes*, author Ray Bradbury uses relative clauses to convey key adjectival information that enhances readers' understandings. This book, which describes the haunted events an October carnival brings to a town, employs the relative clause "where winter slept" in the sentence "Stay away from the maze where winter slept" (p. 123). In this sentence, which discusses the protagonists' experience with the haunted carnival, Bradbury uses a relative clause to provide descriptive information about the maze. Without this clause, the sentence would still make sense on a basic level, but would be without the strong imagery and mood that the ominous relative clause "where winter slept" provides.

A bit later in *Something Wicked This Way Comes*, Bradbury employs a relative clause when discussing the haunted transformation of a man called

Fury to a new and scary figure called the Dwarf: "And in his eyes were the lost bits and fitful pieces of a man named Fury who had sold lightning rods how many days, how many years ago in the long, the easy, the safe and wondrous time before this fright was born" (p. 169). This sentence is particularly relevant to a conversation about this grammatical concept because the relative clause "who had sold lightning rods how many days, how many years ago in the long, the easy, the safe and wondrous time before this fright was born" comprises the majority of the sentence. Without the relative clause, this excerpt would only consist of the statement: "And in his eyes were the lost bits and fitful pieces of a man named Fury." With it, however, the sentence provides a great deal of information about what life was like before, in Bradbury's words, "this fright was born."

These examples from *Something Wicked This Way Comes* illustrate the impact of relative clauses. Without these clauses, the sentences would lack important descriptive information that Bradbury uses to establish the haunting tone that is essential to this novel. Next, let's take a look at the importance of subordinate clauses to effective writing.

Why Are Subordinate Clauses Important to Effective Writing?
Subordinate clauses are tools that writers use to add significant contextual information to the independent clauses they accompany. While an independent clause can exist without a subordinate clause, pairing a subordinate and independent clause can provide a nuanced and descriptive statement that would be much harder to express if the author just used an independent clause. In his 1883 book *Life on the Mississippi*, Mark Twain uses a number of subordinate clauses to provide important contextual and background information. For example, in Chapter 8 of the book, Twain uses a subordinate clause to help readers understand the impressive memory possessed by his mentor, Mr. Bixby: "If he were talking about a trifling letter he had received seven years before, he was pretty sure to deliver you the entire screed from memory" (p. 118). In this sentence, the subordinate clause "if he were talking about a trifling letter he had received seven years before" makes a meaningful contribution to the reader's understanding of the situation. Without this clause, the sentence would only tell us that Mr. Bixby can deliver the contents of a document from memory. With it, however, we understand the trivial nature of the document; this characteristic gives us a full understanding of how impressive Bixby's memory is.

Twain uses another subordinate clause in *Life on the Mississippi* when discussing the preparations associated with steamboat racing. Specifically, Twain explains that careful measures were taken to ensure that boats were loaded with the exact amount of weight that optimized their speed: "If the boat was known to make her best speed when drawing five and a half feet forward and five feet aft, she was carefully loaded to that exact figure—she wouldn't enter a dose of homeopathic pills on her manifest after that" (p. 140). In this sentence, the subordinate clause "if the boat was known to make her best speed when drawing five and a half feet forward and five feet aft" provides an example of the kinds of calculations steamboat pilots took into account when getting their ships ready to race. The concrete information and specific detail conveyed by this subordinate contribute to our understanding of this activity.

As these examples from *Life on the Mississippi* reveal, subordinate clauses are excellent tools for authors to provide contextual details and background information that can greatly contribute to readers' under-standings of the information conveyed in a sentence. In each of these example sentences, the subordinate clauses Twain uses allow us to com-prehend the details surrounding an action or event in a more developed way than if he had chosen not to use this grammatical concept. In the next section, we'll take a look inside a ninth-grade classroom and examine how the students in the class work to understand how and why authors purposefully use relative and subordinate clauses.

A Classroom Snapshot

My excitement is visible; even before all of the ninth graders have reached their seats, I enthusiastically begin today's lesson on clauses and literature. "You all just recently finished *Romeo and Juliet,* and I know you thought about the play in a whole bunch of different ways," I start. "You talked about themes and characters and you made comparisons to current events. One thing that you haven't yet talked about, though, is something we'll examine today: how the grammatical concepts Shakespeare uses have a major impact on the piece by communicating important information to the audience and readers."

Several students nod and a couple sit up in their seats; energized by their interest, I continue: "As you all know, we've been talking recently about relative and subordinate clauses and how each of these types of clauses can have an important effect on a piece of writing. Today, we'll apply our knowledge of these grammatical concepts to the text of *Romeo and Juliet,* examining how Shakespeare uses these clause types to convey important information."

"This is actually really cool," remarks a young lady in the front of the room. "I've never thought about connecting grammar and *Romeo and Juliet* before."

"I'm thrilled to hear that!" I respond. "This is a way to help us think even further about how the concepts of grammar are important tools for effective writing."

In our past few classes, these students and I have been exploring the importance of relative and subordinate clauses to strong writing. First, I introduced them to the fundamental components of these concepts and showed them published sentences containing these clauses. After that, I showed the students revised versions of these sentences with the relative and subordinate clauses removed and talked with them about the impact

Figure 2.3 Clause Analysis Template

Passage Containing a Relative or Subordinate Clause	Type of Clause in Passage	Passage Rewritten without the Clause	Why the Clause Is Important to the Original Passage

the clauses had on the original, published versions of those sentences. Now, in today's class, the students will take on more ownership of their learning by working in small groups to apply their understandings of this grammatical concept to the text of *Romeo and Juliet*: each group of students will select a relative or subordinate clause from the play and analyze its significance to the passage in which it appears.

I explain the activity to my students and then give each group the template they'll complete as they work on the task. This template, depicted in Figure 2.3 and available in reproducible form in Appendix B of this book, asks students to identify a passage from *Romeo and Juliet* that contains either a relative or subordinate clause, state which of these clause types it contains, rewrite the passage without that clause, and explain why the clause is important to the original text.

"I want to show you an example of how to do this before you get started," I tell the students, putting a template on the document camera. "You can see here that I've put on the projector the same template that you'll be using for this activity. One passage from Shakespeare's *Romeo and Juliet* that contains one of these clause types is in Act 5, Scene 1: 'If I may trust the flattering truth of sleep, / My dreams presage some joyful news at hand' (5.1.1–2). Now that I've identified this example, I'll write this passage in the first column on my template. Next, the template asks me about the type of clause in the passage; I'll write 'subordinate clause' here because 'If I may trust the flattering truth of sleep' is an example of a subordinate clause. The third column on the template asks what the passage would be like if it was rewritten without the subordinate clause; for this, I'll write 'My dreams presage some joyful news at hand.'"

"Finally," I continue, "the last column on the template asks me why the clause is important to the original passage. This is a challenging question; to answer it, I need to understand what the whole passage is saying, what the subordinate clause in particular is saying, and why the information expressed in the subordinate clause is significant. Before I write anything for this one, I want to make sure I have a good understanding of all of this information. First of all, I'll think about the passage as a whole. In this part of the play, Romeo is speaking; he's talking about a dream he had in which he died and Juliet's kiss brought him back to life. In this specific passage, Romeo says that, if his dream has some relation to reality, he can expect good news about Juliet. The subordinate clause 'If I may trust the unflattering truth of sleep' is important because it gives explains that there might be some joyful news coming soon, but only if Romeo can trust his dreams. Without it, the statement Romeo makes in the independent clause would seem more certain. I'll write the ideas I just shared about the importance of the subordinate clause in this final column."

"Now, it's your turn!" I exclaim to the students. "Look through *Romeo and Juliet* with your group members and identify a relative or subordinate clause in the play. Then, you can use that clause and the text around it to complete the chart. I'll come around and check in with you while you work."

I give the students some time to get started, circulating the room and listening to their conversations. Once about ten minutes have passed and the student groups are close to completing the activity, I begin to confer with them. I sit down with a group that appears to be finished and ask them what they've discovered.

"We found a subordinate clause that we think is really important," begins a group member.

"That's awesome!" I exclaim. "I love that you not only found a subordinate clause, but also that you think the clause you found is really important to *Romeo and Juliet*. Talk to me about what you noticed."

"We picked out [the passage] 'If you ever disturb our streets again, / Your lives shall pay the forfeit of the peace,'" (1.1.94–95) explains a student in the group.

"Great," I respond. "Now let me know your thoughts on the other information the chart asks for."

"Well, like we said, the passage has a subordinate clause: 'If you ever disturb our streets again,'" replies a student in the group.

"And," interjects another student, "without that clause, it would say, 'Your lives shall pay the forfeit of the peace.'"

"Very nice responses, both of you," I tell the students. "You identified the kind of clause in the passage and shared what the passage would be like if it didn't contain that clause. Now, there's one final thing to consider: why do you think that clause is important to the original passage?"

"Oh, it's really important!" exclaims a student. "The reason it's so important is the Prince is telling Capulet and Montague that they're going to die if they disturb the streets, or fight, again. When the Prince says, 'Your lives shall pay the forfeit of the peace,' he's saying, 'You're going to die.' The subordinate clause tells us why they would die, like what they'd need to do for that to happen to them. It shows how mad the Prince is about the Montagues and Capulets fighting and how serious he is about them stopping."

"That's a fantastic analysis!" I respond. "I love how thoughtfully and carefully you analyzed the significance of this independent clause to the rest of this sentence. You did a really nice job of describing how understanding the independent clause is important to understanding the meaning of what the Prince was staying. Like you describe, this subordinate clause is essential to the Prince getting his message across. Nice work!"

After my conversation with this group, I continue to move around the classroom and check in with the other groups of students, finding myself similarly impressed with their analyses. Before the period ends, I address the class: "You all did an outstanding job today! I am so impressed by how each group not only identified the relative or subordinate clauses in the passages you selected, but also provided really strong insights into the importance of those clauses. You're really learning how grammatical concepts such as these clauses can be used by authors as tools for effective writing—I'm very proud of your work!"

Instructional Recommendations

In this section, I describe a step-by-step instructional process to use when teaching students about the strategic and purposeful uses of subordinate and relative clauses. The instructional steps I recommend are: 1) Present students with published examples of subordinate and relative clauses and discuss the importance of those clauses; 2) Show students published examples with these clauses removed and talk with them about the differences; 3) Ask students to work collaboratively to identify these clauses in published texts and analyze their significance; 4) Work with students as they apply relative and subordinate clauses to their own writings; and 5) Have students reflect on how these clauses impact their works. These instructional steps are designed to help students understand the impact of relative and subordinate clauses and apply them to their works, so I recommend using the descriptions of these concepts at the beginning of this chapter (such as the information in Figures 2.1 and 2.2) to make sure that that students grasp the key features of these concepts before beginning the instructional process.

1. Present students with published examples of subordinate and relative clauses and discuss the importance of those clauses.

Beginning this instructional sequence by showing students published works containing subordinate and relative clauses provides concrete models of how these concepts look in practice, avoiding the disconnect that comes from students looking at grammatical concepts in isolate and emphasizing the authentic ways authors use subordinate and relative clauses in their works. I recently shared with my ninth graders the examples from *Something Wicked This Way Comes* and *Life on the Mississippi* previously described in this chapter. When doing this with your students, I encourage you to use these examples and talk with the students about the impact the subordinate and relative clauses in them have on the piece. In addition, it's also a good idea to find some examples of these grammatical concepts in books that your students particularly enjoy, as this can further increase their engagement.

When presenting published examples of subordinate and relative clauses to your students, I suggest emphasizing that you're showing them those examples to help them understand that these concepts are used in authentic scenarios, not just in grammar books. I recently conveyed this information to my students, saying, "Sometimes people think the concepts of grammar 'live' in grammar books; they're present in those books and really nowhere else. In reality, that couldn't be further from the truth. These concepts 'live' in real writing, like the examples from Bradbury and Twain you see here. Authors use grammatical concepts like the subordinate and relative clauses to make their works as strong as they can."

2. Show students published examples with these clauses removed and talk with them about the differences.

This second step of the instructional process is designed to give students a deeper understanding of the impact of subordinate and relative clauses. When I recently conducted this activity with my students, I displayed the published examples of relative and subordinate clauses from *Something Wicked This Way Comes* and *Life on the Mississippi* I used in the first step alongside revised versions of those examples that no longer contained the clauses we were studying. For example, I juxtaposed the sentence "And in his eyes were the lost bits and fitful pieces of a man named Fury who had sold lightning rods how many days, how many years ago in the long, the easy, the safe and wondrous time before this fright was born" (p. 169) from *Something Wicked This Way Comes* with a revised version without the relative clause. Figure 2.4 depicts the chart I showed the students to illustrate the differences in these sentences. (A blank, reproducible version of this chart is available in Appendix B.)

After displaying the original and revised versions of a sentence with a relative or subordinate clause, I ask students to think about the differences in the information the sentences convey. For example, when I showed my students the two passages depicted in Figure 2.4, I asked them, "What does the original sentence tell us that the revised version without the relative clause does not?" I was excited that many students were eager to comment; one explained, "The original version gives us a ton of info about Fury before everything went all crazy and scary, like what his job was and how his life was much easier." Another added. "The version with the relative clause lets us know that things used to be safe, but now they're not. That's some important info that we don't get when the relative clause is taken away." These comments, as well as others like them, communicated to me that my students understood the importance of the relative clause to this sentence from *Something Wicked This Way Comes* and were ready to move to the next step of this instructional process.

3. Ask students to work collaboratively to identify these clauses in published texts and analyze their significance.

This third step gives students additional ownership by asking them to work in small groups to find a subordinate or relative clause in a published piece and comment on the significance of that clause to the original text. This chapter's classroom snapshot contains an example of how this activity can look in practice; in it, I asked my students to identify a relative or subordinate clause from *Romeo and Juliet,* which they had just finished reading, and analyze the importance of the clause to the passage in which it originally appeared.

Before engaging your students in this group activity, I recommend modeling an example for them so they understand what identifying and analyzing one of these clauses looks like. For example, in the classroom snapshot, I analyzed the importance of the subordinate clause "If I may trust the flattering truth of sleep" in the passage "If I may trust the

Figure 2.4 Sentence Juxtaposition Chart: Relative and Subordinate Clauses

Sentence Containing a Subordinate or Relative Clause	Revised Version without the Subordinate or Relative Clause
"And in his eyes were the lost bits and fitful pieces of a man named Fury who had sold lightning rods how many days, how many years ago in the long, the easy, the safe and wondrous time before this fright was born" (Bradbury, 1962, p.169).	"And in his eyes were the lost bits and fitful pieces of a man named Fury."

flattering truth of sleep, / My dreams presage some joyful news at hand" (5.1.1–2). After I thought aloud for my students on the significance of this clause to the original passage and was confident that they understood the ideas I shared, I told them that it was their turn to conduct a similar analysis by working in groups to identify and comment on the importance of a relative or subordinate clause in *Romeo and Juliet*.

I recommend giving each student group the chart depicted in Figure 2.3 to help them analyze the clause the group members identify. This chart, found earlier in this chapter, guides students through this activity by asking them to write down a passage containing a relative or subordinate clause, state which one of these clause types is present, rewrite the passage without the clause, and finally comment on why the clause is important to the original passage. Once students have this chart and a copy of the text to use, you can give the students some time to work, checking in with them as necessary. After several minutes of collaborative work time have passed, I like to sit down with each student group and hear about their work. One group of ninth graders with which I conferred selected a passage containing a relative clause: this selection, spoken by Lady Capulet when she is trying to convince Juliet to consider marrying Paris, reads, "By my count, I was your mother much upon these years that you are a maid" (1.3.71–73). In their analysis, the group identified the relative clause "that you are a maid," explaining its importance to the original passage by asserting, "this relative clause is important because Lady Capulet uses it to compare herself to Juliet. She's basically saying that Juliet isn't married—she's a maid—and she [Lady Capulet] was a mom at the same age Juliet is now. The relative clause 'that you are a maid' shows this difference between them."

4. Work with students as they apply relative and subordinate clauses to their own writings.

This fourth step of the instructional process is one of the most meaningful and exciting: it provides students with the opportunity to use these grammatical concepts in their own works and allows us teachers to confer and work with them as they do so. Many high school English teachers have shared with me their beliefs that a major flaw in grammar instruction is the lack of application to student writing. "Usually," one ninth grade teacher recently told me, "when we get a grammar program, there's nothing to really help students use what they've learned in the writing they do. It's important for students to be able to see how they can use the grammar they learn in their writing."

I agree with this teacher's statement about the importance of students understanding how they can apply grammatical concepts they learn to the pieces of writing they create. To help students implement their knowledge of relative and subordinate clause in their works, I ask them to keep these grammatical tools in mind as they create new pieces of writing and while they revise existing works. I recently explained this to my ninth graders: "You can use relative and subordinate clauses to add important details and information if you're drafting a new piece. If you're revising a work, you can use these grammatical concepts at that stage as well by looking over what you've written and seeing if there are any places in your writing that seem to be lacking important details. If there are, consider if a relative or subordinate clause might give you the kind of detail that will make that section as strong as possible."

While my students do this, I confer with them individually to monitor their understanding and implementation of these concepts. During these one-on-one meetings, I focus primarily on whether or not the students are using the concepts purposefully, with a clear understanding of how these grammatical components can enhance a piece of work. I explain to them, "It's not good to just use these grammatical concepts just to use them. You only want to use them if they'll provide information that will enhance your work." I recently met with a student who purposefully implemented relative and subordinate clauses in a description of the strategies he uses when playing the football-themed video game *Madden 17*. In this piece, the student integrated the subordinate clause "since they have a good quarterback and a great receiver and the relative clauses "that your opposition cannot stop," "who is the most unstoppable receiver in the game," and "that most teams cannot stop" to help convey his tactics for succeeding in this video game. Figure 2.5 contains an excerpt from this student's work that contains these grammatical concepts.

Figure 2.5 Student Work Excerpt Containing Relative and Subordinate Clauses

The key to being successful in playing *Madden 17* is to figure out what strengths your team has that your opposition cannot stop and then capitalize on those strengths. There are a lot of different strengths your team can possess—for example, you might have an elusive running back or a powerful group of linebackers. Since they have a good quarterback and a great wide receiver, I've found the Pittsburgh Steelers are a hard team for the opposition to defend. The Steelers have a strong-armed quarterback in Ben Roethlisberger; he can throw to wide receiver Antonio Brown, who is the most unstoppable receiver in the game. The combination of Roethlisberger and Brown gives the Steelers a great strength that most teams cannot stop.

5. Have students reflect on how these clauses impact their works.

This final step helps students enhance their understandings of how these concepts contribute to the effectiveness of their works. While one could simply conclude this instructional sequence with the preceding activity of students applying relative and subordinate clauses to the pieces they create, this step takes the process one step further by giving students an opportunity to reflect on why these concepts are important to their writings. To guide my students' reflections on the importance of these concepts to their works, I ask them three related questions: 1) Which clause type or types did you use in your piece?; 2) How do you feel the clauses you used enhanced the piece?; and 3) What would be different about the piece if you had not used these clauses?

I posed these questions to the student who created the piece about strategies to use in the *Madden 17* video game; in response to the first two, he explained, "I used a subordinate clause and three relative clauses in [the piece]. I think they both helped make it more detailed. The subordinate clause 'since they have a good quarterback and a great wide receiver' gives details about why I use the Steelers. It explains what their strengths are and what makes them so good. The first relative clause I used, 'that your opposition cannot stop,' explains what kind of strengths you should look for when playing the game. The second one, 'who is the most unstoppable receiver in the game,' describes exactly how good Antonio Brown is. He's the main reason the Steelers are so good in this game. The third one, 'that most teams cannot stop,' gives information about the strength of the Steelers I'm discussing and why this strength makes them so good."

This student then commented on how the piece would be different if he had not incorporated these grammatical concepts: "Without this subordinate clause and these relative clauses, I wouldn't give as much detail about why I choose to use the Steelers when I play *Madden 17* and what makes them so good. You'd still know the basic information, like the fact that I like to play with the Steelers and that they have Roethlisberger and Brown, but you wouldn't know how good they are if I didn't use these clauses. The piece definitely wouldn't be as good without [these clauses]."

Final Thoughts on Purposefully Using Key Clauses to Convey Specific Meanings and Add Variety

◆ The purposeful use of key clauses to enhance the quality of a piece of writing is included in Common Core Language Standard L.9–10.1.

◆ Two especially significant types of clauses that can make an impact on a piece of writing are relative and subordinate clauses.
  ◆ A relative clause is a dependent clause used to describe a noun in a sentence. These clauses can begin with either relative pronouns (who, whose, whom, which, and that) or relative adverbs (where, when, and why).
  ◆ A subordinate clause is a dependent clause that begins with a subordinating conjunction (such as if, since, although, because, and until) and provides additional context and detail about the information in an independent clause.
◆ Relative and subordinate clauses enhance written works in ways that are unique to their respective attributes.
  ◆ Relative clauses are important to effective writing because they can provide adjectival information that allows readers to reach more developed understandings of people, places, things, and ideas in a text.
  ◆ Subordinate clauses can add significant contextual information to the independent clauses they accompany.
◆ When teaching students about the purposeful use of subordinate and relative clauses:
  ◆ Present students with published examples of subordinate and relative clauses and discuss the importance of those clauses.
  ◆ Show students published examples with these clauses removed and talk with them about the differences.
  ◆ Ask students to work collaboratively to identify these clauses in published texts and analyze their significance.
  ◆ Work with students as they apply relative and subordinate clauses to their own writings.
  ◆ Have students reflect on how these clauses impact their works.

3

Use Semicolons to Link Closely Related Independent Clauses

Now let's examine another grammatical tool that authors implement to maximize the effectiveness of their works: the use of semicolons to link closely related independent clauses. We'll begin by considering how semicolons are used, and then think about why they're important to effective writing. After that, we'll look inside a tenth-grade classroom and notice how the students in that class are learning about the significance of this grammatical concept. We'll close by thinking about some key recommendations to remember when teaching your students about the strategic use of semicolons in writing.

What Is It?

A semicolon is a punctuation mark used to connect independent clauses; the Common Core State Standards highlights the significance of this concept, as Standard L.9–10.2.A calls for students to use them "to link two or more closely related independent clauses" (Core Standards, 2010). To fully understand the features of semicolons, it's important to consider what independent clauses are: an independent clause is a group of words containing a subject and a verb that is able to stand alone as a sentence. For example, the sentence "Jeff is playing baseball this season; he is the starting shortstop" uses a semicolon to link the independent clauses "Jeff is playing baseball this season" and "he is the starting shortstop." Semicolons are typically found in two kinds of sentences: compound sentences, which contain two or more independent clauses, and compound-complex sentences, which contain at least two independent clauses and at least one dependent clause. The preceding sentence "Jeff is playing baseball this season; he is the starting shortstop" is a compound sentence, as it contains two independent clauses. A related compound-complex sentence featuring a semicolon is "Since Jeff started at shortstop, the whole family went to today's baseball game; everyone had a great time," as it contains a dependent clause and two independent clauses. Whether used in a compound or compound-complex sentence, semicolons are used to link related independent clauses such as the ones featured in these examples. Figure 3.1 describes key information about semicolons.

Why Is This Concept Important to Effective Writing?

Semicolons are important tools writers can use to enhance the flow in their works. There are two main ways semicolons maximize the sense of flow in a piece of writing: they link short, choppy sentences and eliminate the need for extra language. Let's look at each of these benefits individually.

Semicolons Link Short, Choppy Sentences

Numerous short, choppy sentences can make a piece difficult to read, as they may interrupt the piece's sense of continuity. While there are times when authors might want to use a concise sentence to communicate a piece of information succinctly and directly, writers frequently look for ways to combine the ideas in shorter sentences, forming longer ones that are easier to read than a series of brief ones. Authors often implement semicolons for this purpose, using them to link independent clauses that convey related information. For example, the sentence "Jeff is playing baseball this season; he is the starting shortstop" described earlier in this chapter uses a semicolon to link what may otherwise be two short, choppy sentences; without the semicolon, this text could read "Jeff is playing baseball this season. He is the starting shortstop."

Figure 3.1 Key Semicolon Information

Grammatical Concept	Semicolon
What is a semicolon?	A semicolon is a punctuation mark used to join independent clauses. It looks like this ;
Where are semicolons found?	Semicolons are typically found in compound and compound-complex sentences.
What do they look like in sentences?	"Jeff is playing baseball this season; he is the starting shortstop." (This is an example of a compound sentence.)
	"Since Jeff started at shortstop, the whole family went to today's baseball game; everyone had a great time." (This is an example of a compound-complex sentence.)

Published authors also use this tool to increase the readability of their works: in his (1960) book *Night*, Elie Wiesel uses semicolons at multiple points in the text to link what would otherwise be short, choppy sentences. When describing the prevailing attitude in the neighborhood he and his family were required to live, Wiesel states, "The people's morale was not too bad; we were beginning to get used to the situation" (p. 18). If this sentence were written as "The people's morale was not too bad. We were beginning to get used to the situation," it would have a much more stilted tone than it currently does, lacking the flow that Wiesel creates in his original text. Shortly afterward in *Night*, Wiesel again uses a semicolon to maximize the readability of his work. While discussing his experience arriving at a concentration camp, Wiesel explains, "Through the windows we could see barbed wire; we realized this must be the camp" (p. 25). By linking these related statements with a semicolon, Wiesel produces a much smoother and easier-to-read sentence than he would have if he had created two short, choppy sentences instead.

Semicolons Eliminate the Need for Extra Language
In addition to linking short, choppy independent clauses, semicolons can eliminate the need for authors to use unnecessary language in their sentences: the most frequently used alternative to incorporating a semicolon to link independent clauses is to use a comma and a coordinating conjunction. (The coordinating conjunctions, sometimes abbreviated as FANBOYS, are *for, and, nor, but, or, yet,* and *so*). While there's nothing wrong with using commas and coordinating conjunctions to combine independent clauses, semicolons give writers a succinct way to establish this same connection without adding extra words to their pieces. For example, the sentences from *Night* discussed in the last section could include coordinating conjunctions such as "for" and "so" if Wiesel did not use semicolons in those passages. The sentence "The people's morale was not too bad; we were beginning to get used to the situation" may read "The people's morale was not too bad, for we were beginning to get used to the situation." Similarly, the sentence "Through the windows we could see barbed wire; we realized this must be the camp" could read "Through the windows we could see barbed wire, so we realized this must be the camp." Wiesel could have chosen to use semicolons or coordinating conjunctions in these sentences; either structure would be correct, but his stylistic choices here demonstrate the concise passages that semicolons can help craft.

As these examples from *Night* illustrate, semicolons are useful tools authors can implement to link short, choppy sentences in their works and eliminate excess language while doing so. In the next section, we'll take a look inside a tenth-grade classroom and see how the students in that class work to understand the significance of this tool to effective writing.

A Classroom Snapshot

"You all have never studied semicolons in this way, have you?" I ask my tenth graders at the beginning of class, a smile across my face.

"No, this has definitely been different from anything we've done before with semicolons," answers a student. "I've never really thought about how semicolons are used in published writing and why they're important—I was just taught what they were."

These students and I are in our third meeting discussing the importance of semicolons to effective writing. In our first conversation about this writing tool, I reviewed the fundamental features of semicolons, showed students published examples of this concept, and talked with them about why the semicolons used by the authors of those examples are important to the effectiveness of their works. Next, in our second meeting on the topic, the students and I discussed how published examples containing semicolons would be different if their authors did not use semicolons, focusing on differences in their flow, structure, and readability.

"Today," I explain to the class, "we're going to get even more interactive in our work with semicolons." I proceed to tell the students about the group activity we're doing. "In this activity, you're going to work with the group in which you're seated and select a book: this book can be from the classroom library or one of your independent books. Once you've decided on the book your group will use, you and group members will pick from two possible activities. One option is to select a passage from the book that uses a semicolon and analyze why the semicolon is important to the effectiveness of that passage. The other option is to identify a passage from a book that doesn't include a semicolon but could—such as a compound sentence or two short, choppy sentences—and revise it so that it includes a semicolon instead. I'm going to give each group two graphic organizers: you'll use the first one if you choose the activity in which you select a passage that uses a semicolon and analyze it; you'll use the second graphic organizer if you choose the activity in which you find a passage that doesn't contain a semicolon and revise it to include one."

I place each of these graphic organizers on the document camera, projecting them to the front of the room so that students can see them, and explain what each one asks the students do to. (Figure 3.2 depicts the graphic organizer associated with the first activity; Figure 3.3 contains the organizer related to the second activity. Reproducible versions of these figures are available in Appendix B.)

Figure 3.2 Graphic Organizer for Semicolon Analysis Activity

Book Used	Passage Containing a Semicolon	How the Passage Could Be Written without the Semicolon	Why the Semicolon Is Important to the Original Passage

After describing what each graphic organizer asks for, I tell the students that I'm going to show them some examples of what this activity can look like. "I want to show you what both of these activities can look like in practice so that you have clear understandings of what to do when you do this with your group members. One book that I really enjoy is *The Namesake* by Jhumpa Lahiri (2003), and I know a number of you have read it for independent reading and enjoyed it as well, so I've brought in some sentences from that book that are related to this activity."

"For the first activity option," I continue, "the one that asks you to find a passage with a semicolon, I've selected the following sentence from *The Namesake*, which describes how people called for help after a train accident: 'The train guard's portable phone would not work; it was only after the guard ran nearly five kilometers from the site of the accident, to Ghatshila, that he was able to transmit the first message for help' (p. 17). Now, the next column on the chart asks how the passage could be written without its semicolon; one way is to include a comma and a coordinating conjunction such as 'and.' This would create the sentence, 'The train guard's portable phone would not work, and it was only after the guard ran nearly five kilometers from the site of the accident, to Ghatshila, that he was able to transmit the first message for help.' Finally, let's look at the final column on the chart, which asks why the semicolon is important to the original passage. I think the semicolon is important to that sentence in *The Namesake* because it connects two related sentences

Figure 3.3 Graphic Organizer for Semicolon Revision Activity

Book Used	Original Passage	How the Passage Could Be Revised to Include a Semicolon	How Incorporating a Semicolon Changes the Original Passage

and eliminates the need for the conjunction 'and' while connecting them. If I couldn't use a semicolon here, I'd either have two short, choppy sentences or I'd have to use an extra word to link them. The semicolon creates a situation in which I don't have to do either of these things."

Students around the classroom nod and indicate their understanding; I proceed to describe an example of the second activity. "For this activity," I explain, "I've selected a sentence from *The Namesake* that does not contain a semicolon, but could be revised to include one. The sentence, which describes the setting of a hospital room, reads, 'The lights are soothingly dim, and there is only one other bed next to hers, empty for the time being' (p. 22). In this sentence, there are two sections that could stand on their own, called independent clauses. They are 'The lights are soothingly dim' and 'there is only one other bed next to hers, empty for the time being.' Since these are the sentence's two independent clauses, we could revise it to include a semicolon by writing, 'The lights are soothingly dim; there is only one other bed next to hers, empty for the time being.' In this new version, I've placed a semicolon between the two independent clauses. The final step of this activity is to comment on how incorporating a semicolon changes the original passage. In this situation, incorporating a semicolon changes the original text by eliminating the coordinating conjunction 'and.' I believe that eliminating this conjunction makes the sentence less wordy."

Once I've modeled these examples and activities for the students, I tell them it's time for them to work with their group members on one of these two activities. I give each group some time to work together;

while they do so, I move around in the classroom, listening to the groups discuss and analyze the examples they've selected. After a few more minutes have passed and it seems like some of the groups are starting to finish up, I sit down with a student group and ask them about their work.

"How are things going?" I ask the students.

"Great," answers a group member. "We did the first activity, the one where we find something containing a semicolon, rewrite it without the semicolon, and say why the semicolon is important."

"Wonderful," I respond. "What book did you select?"

"We used the book *A Lesson Before Dying*," (Gaines, 1993) replies another student in the group.

"Great choice!" I interject.

"Thanks," continues the student. "We read it earlier in the year and we remembered some times when the author used semicolons, so we thought it would be good for this. The sentence we picked out is, 'I didn't want to think about that cell uptown; I didn't even want to think about Miss Emma and the lies I had to tell her' (p. 90). There's a semicolon between 'uptown' and 'I.'"

"Nice job identifying that example and stating where the semicolon is," I assert. "How could you write that sentence without a semicolon?"

"We rewrote it as 'I didn't want to think about that cell uptown, and I didn't even want to think about Miss Emma and the lies I had to tell her,'" answers a group member.

"Good work," I respond. "I see that you included the coordinating conjunction 'and' in that example. Now, tell me about your thoughts on the topic in the last column: why do you think the semicolon is important to the original passage?"

"We said the semicolon's important," replies a student in the group, "because you don't need to use 'and' when you use the semicolon. We think the sentence sounds better without 'and.' The semicolon makes it sound smoother."

"Wonderful job!" I exclaim. "You all did such a great job of thoughtfully analyzing the importance of the semicolon to the sense of flow in the original sentence from that book."

Once I complete my conversation with this group, I continue to circulate around the classroom, talking with the other student groups. Some other groups have selected the first activity option, while others have picked the second one, in which they identify a passage that doesn't incorporate a semicolon but could and revise it to include one. After I've spoken with each group, I praise the class's outstanding work: "Each of our groups did such great work today! I am particularly impressed by how carefully each group thought about the importance of the semicolon to the passage you selected or the revised version you created. Awesome stuff!"

Instructional Recommendations

In this section, I describe a step-by-step instructional process to use when teaching students about effective semicolon use. The instructional steps I recommend are: 1) Show students examples of published sentences that contain semicolons and discuss the importance of the semicolons to those sentences; 2) Talk with students about how those published examples would be different if their authors did not use semicolons; 3) Have students work collaboratively to analyze the significance of semicolon use; 4) Ask students to apply the writing tool of semicolons to their own works; and 5) Enable students to reflect on how the semicolons they use impact their pieces. These steps are designed to help students apply their knowledge of semicolons by considering the importance of this grammatical concept to effective writing; I suggest using the information at the beginning of this chapter (such as the details presented in Figure 3.1) to make sure students grasp the fundamental aspects of semicolons before launching the instructional process.

1. Show students examples of published sentences that contain semicolons and discuss the importance of the semicolons to those sentences.

This initial step is important because it places the grammatical concept of semicolons in the realm of authentic, published writing. Oftentimes, students only see punctuation-related concepts such as semicolons in textbooks and on worksheets; I've found that showing students how published authors use this punctuation tool can go a long way toward making instruction relevant and engaging. When I initially told my tenth graders that we'd be spending the upcoming class periods talking about semicolons, they seemed surprised that we'd spend so much time talking about a punctuation mark. However, once I showed them published examples of this concept and led discussions about its significance to effective writing, they understood that we would be looking at semicolons differently and more analytically then they had before.

When doing this with my students, I showed them the examples from *Night* described earlier in this chapter—"The people's morale was not too bad; we were beginning to get used to the situation" (p. 18) and "Through the windows we could see barbed wire; we realized this must be the camp" (p. 25)—and talked with them about how the semicolons in each of these sentences allow the author to link short independent clauses and to avoid the use of coordinating conjunctions while doing so. During this conversation, I emphasized that authors don't always choose to use semicolons, noting that authors can certainly opt to have short independent clauses stand on their own in or use coordinating conjunctions to link those clauses. I did, however, make sure students understood the key benefits of semicolons: they are useful tools that link short, choppy sentences and eliminate the need for extra language.

2.   Talk with students about how those published examples would be different if their authors did not use semicolons.

This step of the instructional process builds off the first one and is designed to get students thinking even more analytically about the importance of semicolons to effective writing. To help students understand how published examples would be different without semicolons, I like to show them a chart that includes three pieces of information: the original text of each example we discuss, how that sentence would look if it were rewritten as two separate sentences, and how it would look if it were rewritten with a comma and a coordinating conjunction linking independent clauses instead of a semicolon. Juxtaposing these constructions can help students understand the choices authors have when working with related independent clauses by giving them clear visual representations of the impact semicolons can have. Figure 3.4 depicts a chart I recently showed my students when discussing the sentences from *Night* described in this chapter. (A blank, reproducible version of this chart is available in Appendix B.)

While displaying this chart on the document camera and sharing with students the sentence constructions on it, I emphasized the differences in the versions of each sentence. I've found that students benefit from being able to see how much of an impact semicolon use has on the construction of a sentence; at the end of a discussion on this topic,

Figure 3.4 Comparisons of Sentences with and without Semicolons

Original Text	Revision One: Revised to Create Separate Sentences	Revision Two: Revised with a Comma and Coordinate Conjunction Instead of a Semicolon
"The people's morale was not too bad; we were beginning to get used to the situation" (Wiesel, 1960, p. 18).	The people's morale was not too bad. We were beginning to get used to the situation.	The people's morale was not too bad, for we were beginning to get used to the situation.
"Through the windows we could see barbed wire; we realized this must be the camp" (Wiesel, 1960, p. 25).	Through the windows we could see barbed wire. We realized this must be the camp.	Through the windows we could see barbed wire, so we realized this must be the camp.

one student shared with me that looking at the differences in each of these sentences helped her comprehend the impact of semicolons: "Looking at these different sentences was a huge help! Now I really get how much using a semicolon can change the way a sentence was put together."

3. Have students work collaboratively to analyze the significance of semicolon use.

At this stage in the instructional process, I like for students to take increased responsibility for their learning by working together to put their knowledge of semicolons into action. I recommend facilitating students' analysis by creating an interactive activity in which student groups can choose from two options: they can identify a sentence from a published text that contains a semicolon and analyze the significance of the semicolon to the sentence, or they select a passage that doesn't contain a semicolon, revise it to include one, and comment on how incorporating a semicolon changes the original passage. This chapter's classroom snapshot describes my experience conducting this activity with my students. As discussed in the snapshot, I recommend modeling for your students how you would conduct each of these activities before asking them to do so. Once you've shown your students how to complete these tasks, you can give them the graphic organizers depicted in Figures 3.2 and 3.3 and ask them to work together to select a text and an activity option.

When working with the tenth-grade class mentioned in the classroom snapshot, I met with a group of students who selected a compound sentence from a biography of Thomas Jefferson by Joseph J. Ellis titled *American Sphinx* (1996), revised it to contain a semicolon, and analyzed how the incorporation of a semicolon revised the passage. One of the students in the group had used the book previously for a research project and found it well-written and interesting. The group members chose a sentence from a section describing Jefferson's inauguration: "All the seats on the Senate floor were filled, and the gallery was crowded to capacity" (p. 205). The revised version that they created omitted the coordinating conjunction "and," replacing the comma after "filled" with a semicolon: "All the seats on the Senate floor were filled; the gallery was crowded to capacity." Finally, the group explained that incorporating a semicolon changed the original text: "The semicolon changes it because now the sentence doesn't have to use 'and' to show the connection between the two statements. The sentence still shows that the statements are connected and still puts them together in the sentences, but now it doesn't need to use the word 'and' to do it."

4. Ask students to apply the writing tool of semicolons to their own works.

This instructional step gives students even more responsibility by asking them to use semicolons strategically and purposefully in their own writings. Before students work on applying this concept to their pieces, I like to give them some final reminders to ensure their effective use of this concept: "Just because you know how to use semicolons doesn't mean you need to use them in every sentence," I'll tell them. "Sometimes, it's better to use a short sentence if you want to ensure that readers focus on each point separately. Also, sometimes you might want to use a coordinating conjunction instead of a semicolon when linking related independent clauses; semicolons are *a* tool writers use, but they're not the only tool they can for this reason."

As the students work, I meet with them individually, monitoring their use of the concept and providing any reinforcement necessary. In these one-on-one meetings, I ask students to show me any examples of semicolons they've used in their pieces; I use these examples to evaluate how well students have implemented this writing tool. I recently worked with a student who included a semicolon in a piece he was writing about the character in literature with whom he most relates. Figure 3.5 conveys an excerpt from this student's piece; he uses a semicolon between the words "nicely" and "I" in the third sentence to connect information about how he and Nick Carraway in *The Great Gatsby* both appreciate genuine kindness and reject superficiality.

5. Enable students to reflect on how the semicolons they use impact their pieces.

The final step of this instructional process calls for students to consider the impact of the semicolons they used on the pieces they created. I suggest helping students reflect on the importance of this concept by asking

Figure 3.5 Student Work Excerpt Featuring Semicolon Use

The character from literature that I most relate to is Nick Carraway from *The Great Gatsby*. Nick and I are both loyal and honest people who don't appreciate it when others are superficial. Nick stops spending time with people like Jordan Baker and Tom Buchanan when he realizes they're just concerned with their social status and not with treating others nicely; I stopped hanging out with some individuals in my class when it became clear to me that they were only nice to the people who would get them invited to the cool parties.

them two related questions: 1) How did the semicolons you used enhance your piece?; and 2) How would your piece be different if you had not used them?

I posed these reflection questions to the student who created the piece featured in Figure 3.5. In response to the first question, he explained, "The semicolon I used helped the essay because it connected the statements I made about how Nick Carraway acts and how I act. These sentences are related, so I wanted to connect them, and the semicolon let me do that without using extra words." This student then commented on how the piece would be different without semicolons: "If I didn't use this semicolon, I would either have to rewrite the sentence as two separate ones or use an extra word in the sentence. I like the sentence better with a semicolon. I think making it into two short ones would be too choppy, and adding extra words might not sound as good as it does." These statements reveal an impressive awareness of the impact that the semicolon the student used had on his piece; in addition, his responses suggest an even larger awareness of the significance of this concept to effective writing in general. This kind of deep and thoughtful understanding of the importance of a grammatical component is representative of effective grammar instruction.

Final Thoughts on Purposefully Using Semicolons to Link Closely Related Independent Clauses

- ◆ The purposeful use of semicolons to link closely related independent clauses is addressed in Common Core Language Standard L.9–10.2.A.
- ◆ Semicolons are typically found in two kinds of sentences: compound sentences, which contain two or more independent clauses, and compound-complex sentences, which contain at least two independent clauses and at least one dependent clause.
- ◆ There are two main benefits associated with the use of semicolons in writing:
  - ◆ Semicolons link short, choppy sentences.
  - ◆ Semicolons eliminate the need for extra language.
- ◆ When teaching students about the purposeful and strategic use of semicolons:
  - ◆ Show students examples of published sentences that contain semicolons and discuss the importance of the semicolons to those sentences.
  - ◆ Talk with students about how those published examples would be different if their authors did not use semicolons.

- ◆ Have students work collaboratively to analyze the significance of semicolon use.
- ◆ Ask students to apply the writing tool of semicolons to their own works.
- ◆ Enable students to reflect on how the semicolons they use impact their pieces.

4

Interpret Figures of Speech and Understand Their Roles in a Text

In this chapter, we'll consider the importance of figures of speech to effective writing. First, we'll identify some especially useful and widely used figures of speech and then reflect on why they can enhance a written work. The next step will be for us to take a look inside a tenth-grade classroom where my students will be working to enhance their understandings of figures of speech. Finally, we'll consider key recommendations to keep in mind when helping your students grasp this concept.

What Is It?

Figures of speech—words and phrases used for effect that provide alternatives to straightforward expressions—are tools authors use to enhance the impact of their pieces. The Common Core State Standards emphasize the importance of this concept; Standard L.9–10.5.A explains that students should "interpret figures of speech (e.g., euphemism, oxymoron) in context and analyze their role in the text" (Core Standards, 2010). Let's begin our exploration of this strategy by considering some particularly important and popular types of figures of speech: euphemism, oxymoron, and hyperbole. Common Core Standard L.9–10.5.A specifically identifies the concepts of euphemism and oxymoron as examples of figures of speech that students should understand; I've also selected hyperbole for inclusion in this chapter because of its prevalence in high-school level writing. We'll take a look at each of these figures of speech individually.

Euphemism

A euphemism is a figure of speech used to provide a gentler and more pleasant-sounding replacement for a statement that may feel harsh and

Figure 4.1 Key Information about Euphemism, Oxymoron, and Hyperbole

Figure of Speech	Description	Examples
Euphemism	A figure of speech used to provide a gentler and more pleasant-sounding replacement for a statement that may feel harsh and offensive.	"pass away" (in place of die) "let go" (in place of fire from a job)
Oxymoron	The pairing of words or phrases that seem contradictory.	"deafening silence" "alone together"
Hyperbole	A figure of speech in which a statement is intentionally exaggerated for impact.	"My backpack weighs a ton." "I haven't eaten in hours, and I'm starving!"

offensive. Some especially common euphemism examples are "pass away" (in place of die) and "let go" (in place of fire from a job). In the context of full sentences, these euphemism examples could read "They passed away last year" or "The company had to reduce its size and many good employees needed to be let go."

Oxymoron

An oxymoron is the pairing of words or phrases that seem contradictory. For example, the description "deafening silence" is an oxymoron. "Deafening" and "silence" have opposite meanings; when paired together like this, they form a descriptor that refers to a particular meaningful silence. If a writer said, "The mayor expected applause after her speech; instead, it was met with deafening silence," the oxymoron would convey the significance of this silence. Another oxymoron example is the phrase "alone together"; typically, these words have opposite meanings: people can either be "alone" or they can be "together." When used in conjunction with each other, these words form an oxymoron that can mean that two people are together without anyone else in their presence, such as "At the crowded gathering, the couple had few opportunities to be alone together."

Hyperbole

Hyperbole is a figure of speech in which a statement is intentionally exaggerated for impact. For example, a student might say, "My backpack weighs a ton" to communicate that she is carrying a very heavy backpack. The speaker wouldn't actually be stating that the backpack weighs 2,000 pounds, but rather would be expressing that her backpack is extremely heavy. Another example of hyperbole is found in the sentence: "I haven't eaten in hours, and I'm starving!" In this sentence, the statement "I'm starving" is meant to express that the speaker is very hungry, but not actually that he is in a state of starvation; this intentional exaggeration to make a point is hyperbole.

Figure 4.1 describes key features and examples of euphemism, oxymoron, and hyperbole.

Why Is This Concept Important to Effective Writing?

Figures of speech such as euphemism, oxymoron, and hyperbole all allow authors to create pieces that align with their audiences and purposes as closely and effectively as possible. Since figures of speech go beyond the literal meaning of language, they give authors important and useful flexibility they may not otherwise have. Because euphemism, oxymoron, and hyperbole all have unique features that impact pieces of writing in distinct ways, we'll look at the importance of each one individually.

Why Is Euphemism Important to Effective Writing?

Euphemism is an important tool for effective writing because it allows authors to use language throughout a work that is consistent with the piece's overall tone. For example, if a writer intends to use formal language throughout a piece of writing, she might employ euphemisms that have a formal-sounding tone to achieve this goal. If an entire work is written formally with the exception of one or two statements, those statements could distract and confuse readers. In *Wuthering Heights,* Emily Brontë (1847) uses euphemisms to keep the formal tone established by Lockwood, the book's initial narrator. When describing a woman named Zillah reprimanding a young man for what she perceived his role to be in a violent incident, Lockwood uses the euphemism "turned her vocal artillery" in place of "yelled," producing the statement "…she turned her vocal artillery against the younger scoundrel" (p. 14). At another point in the text, Lockhart explains that Heathcliff, a major character in the book, did not want to see him again by euphemistically stating, "He evidently wished no repetition of my intrusion" (p. 6). Both of these euphemisms keep the book's formal tone; if the text read "yelled" instead of "turned her vocal artillery" or "He really didn't want me to ever come back" instead of "He evidently wished no repetition of my intrusion," the formal nature of *Wuthering Heights* would not be conveyed as clearly to the reader.

Why Is Oxymoron Important to Effective Writing?

Oxymoron is an important concept for effective writing; this type of figurative language provides authors with the ability to add nuance and complexity to their works. The counterintuitive nature of oxymoron use allows writers to express intricate thoughts that more straightforward language may not allow. For example, in *Romeo and Juliet*, Shakespeare employs oxymoron to illustrate the complexities of Romeo's emotions. Early in the play, when Romeo is frustrated by his failed relationship with Rosaline, he makes oxymoron-laden statements, such as "O heavy lightness, serious vanity" (1.1.168). These contradictory expressions give insight into Romeo's state of confusion at the time; Shakespeare's use of this writing tool helps convey this message to the reader. As Romeo tries to make sense of the world around him and its apparent contradictions, he calls attention to other oxymoronic ideas such as lightness that can, in some way, feel heavy, and situations of vanity or triviality that still have a sense of seriousness to them.

Why Is Hyperbole Important to Effective Writing?

Authors use the concept of hyperbole to provide extra emphasis to statements that are particularly significant. Through the use of hyperbole, authors can intentionally exaggerate a description of an event or action to call readers' attention to its importance. For example, in *The Catcher in the Rye* (1951), J.D. Salinger has narrator and protagonist Holden Caulfield use a number of hyperbolic examples to provide extra emphasis to his statements. Very early in the book, Holden asserts, "…my parents would have about two hemorrhages apiece if I told anything pretty personal about them" (p. 1). It's unlikely that Holden actually feels his parents will experience medical emergencies if he shares personal information about them; instead, he uses hyperbole to explain their attitudes on privacy. Later in the text, Holden makes a hyperbolic observation about the number of school-related notebooks his sister Phoebe possesses: "She has about five thousand notebooks. You never saw a kid with so many notebooks" (p. 177). Both of these observations from Holden Caulfield's narration of *The Catcher in the Rye* are not intended to be taken literally, but instead exaggerate facts to make a point. It's also important to note that these uses of hyperbole align with Holden's witty and sarcastic narrative style; the hyperbolic statements described here are consistent with the attitude and personality Holden exhibits throughout the book.

As these examples from *Wuthering Heights, Romeo and Juliet,* and *The Catcher in the Rye* illustrate, the figurative language concepts of euphemism, oxymoron, and hyperbole are important tools for effective writing: they allow authors to craft statements in careful ways that convey messages as strategically and purposefully as possible. In the next section, we'll take a look inside a tenth-grade English class and observe how I help the students in that class understand these writing strategies.

A Classroom Snapshot

"Before we get started today," I tell my tenth graders at the beginning of our class meeting, "let's talk about what we've done so far with figures of speech. On Monday, we discussed what figures of speech are, talking specifically about euphemism, oxymoron, and hyperbole and looking at examples of each of those concepts in published literature. Then, on Tuesday, we talked about why each of those concepts can be useful to effective writing. So, here's my question for you: what have you noticed so far about our conversations about figures of speech?"

"What's stuck out to me is how you talked about why [euphemism, oxymoron, and hyperbole] are important to good writing," answers a young lady in the front of the class.

"Thanks for that reply," I tell the student. "Why do you think that's stood out to you?"

"I think," she continues, "because no teacher I've had has ever really talked about figures of speech like that before. They talked about what different figures of speech are and gave us quizzes on the different kinds. Some showed examples from books, but no one talked about *why* writers use them."

"That's such an important insight," I reply, "because your comments address the significance of thinking about why writers use euphemism, oxymoron, and hyperbole. It's so important, when thinking about any grammatical concept, to consider why it's important to effective writing."

Next, I introduce the activity we'll engage in that day, explaining that the students will work in small groups to identify and select examples of euphemism, oxymoron, or hyperbole in literature and comment on their significance. As part of this activity, students will complete the graphic organizer depicted in Figure 4.2, which asks them

Figure 4.2 Graphic Organizer for Figure of Speech Analysis Activity

Book Used	Figure of Speech You Identified	How It Appears in the Text	Why the Figure of Speech Is Important to the Passage in which It Appears

to state the text they used for the activity, the figure of speech they identified, how that figure of speech appears in the text, and why they think the figure of speech is important to the passage in which it appears. (A blank, reproducible version of this graphic organizer is available in Appendix B.)

I give each group a copy of the graphic organizer and provide further instruction: "To complete this activity, you can choose a text from the classroom library, a book we've already read as a class, or one that someone in your group has used for independent reading. Before I turn you loose to work on the activity, though, I want to model for you an example of what completing this task can look like."

I place a graphic organizer on the document camera and continue: "For this example, I'm going to use the book *All the King's Men* by Robert Penn Warren (1946), so I'll write the title and author in the first column of the graphic organizer that reads 'Book Used.' The figure of speech I identified from this book for this activity is hyperbole. Let's take a look at how it appears in the text: when describing the hospital that he intends to build, politician Willie Stark hyperbolically states, "Boy, I'll tell you, I'm going to have a cage of canaries in every room that can sing Italian grand opera and there ain't going to be a nurse that hasn't won a beauty contest at Atlantic City and every bedpan will be eighteen-carat gold… (p. 139)." This is an example of hyperbole because Stark is exaggerating for effect: he doesn't really mean to convey that the hospital he plans to build will have opera-singing canaries, pageant-winning nurses, and gold bedpans; instead, he's using these descriptions to assert that he wants to build a high-quality hospital. For the last column on the graphic organizer, which asks me to comment on why the figure of speech—in this case, hyperbole—is important to the passage in which it appears, I'm going to write that the hyperbole is important because it allows Stark to express that he wants to build an amazing hospital and lets him do so in a creative and entertaining way that gets his point across effectively."

"Now," I continue, "it's your turn! I'm going to give you some time to work in your groups to find an example of either euphemism, oxymoron, or hyperbole in a published text and then discuss its importance to the passage in which it appears. I'll circulate and see how you're doing; once some time has passed and you've made progress, I'll sit down with each group and hear what everyone has noticed."

The first group with which I meet is using the book *A Long Way Gone* by Ishmael Beah (2007). "You all have been working hard! Tell me about what you've found."

"We found a euphemism in this book," explains a group member. "We picked the book up off the classroom library shelf and started looking through it; the euphemism just popped out to us."

"That's fantastic!" I reply. "What is the example you identified?"

"It's a euphemism about death, but that makes sense since the book's subtitle is 'Memoirs of a Boy Soldier.' The euphemism is in this sentence on page 99: 'For a few minutes I tried to image what it felt like for Gasemu when his fingers vibrated to let the last air out of his body.' The euphemism is 'let the last air out of his body.' We said the euphemism is important to the sentence because it lets Ishmael Beah use a nicer tone to say someone died. We thought the tone in this sentence was much gentler and nicer than it would be if it said 'his fingers vibrated while he died' instead of the way it's written in the book, 'his fingers vibrated to let the last air out of his body.'"

"Really nice response," I tell the student. "You thoughtfully explained that it makes sense that one would find euphemisms about death in a book about a child soldier and did a nice job of identifying the euphemism in the passage you shared. I especially love how insightful your analysis was: you did a wonderful job of talking about the tone this euphemism creates and how the author likely selected that euphemism to create a gentler tone for the reader. Great job!"

I continue around the classroom, checking in with the other groups; I'm impressed by the range of texts the students have selected and how insightfully each group explains the importance of the figure of speech it has identified to the passage in which that figure of speech appears. Once I've met with each group and provided feedback, I close the class meeting with a final comment: "You all were awesome in today's activity! Each group provided important and thoughtful insights into how the example euphemism, oxymoron, or hyperbole you found is important to the text where you found it. Tomorrow, we're going to take our work with this concept to an even higher level by thinking of ways we can strategically apply it to own writings."

Instructional Recommendations

In this section, I'll share a five-step instructional process to use when teaching your students about the strategic use of euphemism, oxymoron, and hyperbole. The steps of this process are: 1) Show students published examples of euphemism, oxymoron, and hyperbole; 2) Talk with students about how the published examples you've shown them are enhanced by the figures of speech they contain; 3) Ask students to work collaboratively to find examples of these figures of speech and analyze their importance; 4) Have students apply the strategies of euphemism, oxymoron, and hyperbole to their own works; and 5) Facilitate student reflection on the impact of these figures of speech on the pieces they create. These instructional steps are meant to help students apply their knowledge of euphemism, oxymoron, and hyperbole; I recommend utilizing the information at the beginning of this chapter, especially the details in the chart depicted in Figure 4.1, to ensure students grasp the fundamental components of these figures of speech before starting this process.

1. Show students published examples of euphemism, oxymoron, and hyperbole.

This initial step gives students an authentic look at how published authors use euphemism, oxymoron, and hyperbole, emphasizing that these concepts are used in actual works of literature and not just in textbooks and on worksheets. I recently showed my tenth graders the examples from *Wuthering Heights, Romeo and Juliet,* and *The Catcher in the Rye* described in this chapter, explaining to them why I was doing so: "I'm showing you these examples so that you can see that figures of speech like euphemism, oxymoron, and hyperbole are real things that great writers use," I explained. "I don't want you to think that these are just things you need to memorize for a test or quiz and then forget; they're much more important than that. They're useful tools for effective writing; these published authors use them to make their works really strong, and I'm going to teach you to do the same thing in your works." Showing students these published examples sets the stage for the rest of this instructional process, which calls for them to think carefully about the significance of these concepts to the works in which they appear and to writing in general.

2. Talk with students about how the published examples you've shown them are enhanced by the figures of speech they contain.

This step is designed to enhance students' understandings of the importance of euphemism, oxymoron, and hyperbole to effective writing, using the published examples you showed the students in the first step to facilitate this analysis. When I do this with my students, I use the document camera to project each example to the front of the class, identify the figure of speech in each one, and think aloud about why that figure of speech is important to the original passage. For example, in a recent discussion with my tenth graders about the importance of hyperbole to effective writing, I displayed the examples of hyperbole from *The Catcher in the Rye* described in this chapter and explained why I feel these hyperbolic examples enhance the quality of the passages in which they appear.

To help students understand the impact of a figure of speech, I like to explain how the sentence would differ if the figure of speech had not been used. For example, when thinking aloud about the sentence 'She has about five thousand notebooks. You never saw a kid with so many notebooks' from *The Catcher in the Rye*, I explained that, if hyperbole were not used, the text could read, 'My sister has a lot of notebooks.' I then talked with the students about how the original version is more representative of Holden Caulfield's attitude and character than the revised sentence. Similarly, when talking with my students about the impact of euphemisms, I explained that the sentence "He evidently wished no repetition of my intrusion" from *Wuthering Heights* creates a different (and significantly more polite) tone than the possible statement "He really didn't want me to ever come back." When discussing the impact of oxymoron with my students, I use a similar tactic, but also vary the strategy somewhat because of the nature of that figure of speech; an oxymoron isn't an alternative phrasing like euphemism or hyperbole, but instead is a statement containing some level of contradiction. Due to this difference, I help students understand the impact of oxymoron by showing them how a text appears with this figure of speech included and how the piece reads with the oxymoron left out. For example, when describing the importance of the oxymoronic statements "O heavy lightness, serious vanity" to *Romeo and Juliet,* I'll also show them how the same section of the play would read without that statement. This analytical work prepares students for the next step of the instructional process, when they'll take on more responsibility for their analyses.

3. Ask students to work collaboratively to find examples of these figures of speech and analyze their importance.

I feel that students learn best when they are given opportunities to apply their understandings of what they've been taught and that teachers are most effective when giving students chances to put their knowledge into action. The third step of the instructional process is based on this idea; it calls for students to work together to identify examples of euphemism, oxymoron, or hyperbole in published texts and to reflect on why the figure of speech they found is important to the passage in which it appears. I've found that this activity, an example of which is described in this chapter's classroom snapshot, is most successful when I model the activity for the class before asking the students to try it out on their own. This gives the students a clear understanding of how to navigate the steps of the activity and allows me to review key points about euphemism, oxymoron, and hyperbole before students work on the activity.

Once you've modeled the activity for the students, organized them in groups, and given each group a copy of the graphic organizer depicted in Figure 4.2, the students are ready to begin! They can either choose books from the classroom library, as discussed in the classroom snapshot, or can use a specific work you assign, such as one they're currently reading or have recently read as a class. After the students have had a bit of time in their groups to work together on identifying a figure of speech in a text and analyzing its significance to the passage in which it appears, I suggest conferring with each group and asking the students in the groups to talk you through their identification and analysis process.

A group in the class described in the classroom snapshot found an example of hyperbole in *Mrs. Dalloway* (Woolf, 1925): "We picked out this statement here that we thought was hyperbole," explained a group member. "It says '…she was never in the room five minutes without making you feel her superiority, your inferiority…' (p. 11). We thought this was hyperbole because it sounds to us like an exaggeration [used] to make a point. The character probably doesn't really make people feel inferior before five minutes are up. It's probably an exaggeration to show that she acted like that a lot." When asked why they believe this hyperbolic language is important to the effectiveness of the text, a group member explained, "We think it's important because it really shows that this character must make people feel inferior a lot and does so in a way that stands out to you when you read it. This hyperbole gives the statement more impact than it would have if the hyperbole wasn't there."

4. Have students apply the strategies of euphemism, oxymoron, and hyperbole to their own works.

At this point in the process, I like to ask students to incorporate one or more of the figures of speech we've been studying into the pieces they're writing at the time. When I prepare students to do this, I review with them the features and benefits of euphemism, oxymoron, and hyperbole. In addition, I emphasize that writers use these concepts purposefully and only when they are the best tactics to use in specific scenarios, helping students understand that they should use these figures of speech strategically and with clear understandings of the benefits they provide. "You'll only use these when they are relevant and useful to your piece," I tell them. "For example, you don't need to use a euphemism unless it's going to provide some benefit to your work—you don't want to use one just to do so."

While the students work, I meet with them individually, talking with them about instances when they used one or more of these figures of speech. I recently spoke with a student who used several examples of hyperbole in a short story he was writing; he explained that he used hyperbolic language to capture the character of the fictional town in which his story was set: "I used a lot of hyperbole in the first paragraph of this story. I made one of the characters say that the town was so unknown that living there made you more hidden than the witness protection program, and later in the paragraph I made that same character say that there were more stories about the town's famous apple sauce recipe than leaves in a forest. I also wrote in this paragraph that people in the town say that the apple sauce is so good it makes pigs fly and bears sing." Figure 4.3 contains the excerpt from this student's work that makes these hyperbolic statements.

5. Facilitate student reflection on the impact of these figures of speech on the pieces they create.

Now that students have applied figures of speech to their works, I like to conclude the instructional sequence by helping them reflect on how the writing tools they utilized impacted the quality of their works. To guide the students' reflections, I ask them three related questions: 1) What figure (or figures) of speech did you use in your piece?; 2) How do you feel this language impacted the piece?; and 3) How you do think your piece would be different if you did not use the figurative language that you did? I like using these questions because they ask students to consider the figurative language they used in gradually increasing levels of complexity: first by identifying the language they used, second by considering how it strengthened the work, and third by contrasting the existing work with how the piece would look without the figurative language used.

The student who created the work excerpted in Figure 4.3 stated that the hyperbole he used in his piece "impacted it because [the hyperbole] emphasized certain things about the town, like how small it is, how good people think the apple sauce is, and how the people there have so many stories about how the apple sauce recipe came about, which is the mystery that the story's really about." This student then continued to explain another way the hyperbole in the piece made a difference: "I think it also impacted the story because it showed the personality of the people in the town. Like, since they're exaggerating things and using hyperbole, you can tell they're kind of creative and interesting and definitely not boring people." In response to the question of how the piece would be different without hyperbole, the student asserted, "I think it definitely wouldn't be as interesting to read. It

Figure 4.3 Student Work Excerpt Featuring Hyperbole

The town of Harris Pass, a small Virginia community at the foot of the Blue Ridge Mountains, isn't particularly well-known. "You can live here and be more hidden than if you were in the witness protection program," Mr. Smith, who runs the town's general store, likes to say. However, people who live in Harris Pass are especially proud of the town's outstanding apple sauce, which has been said to make pigs fly and bears sing. While everyone in Harris Pass can agree the apple sauce in town is amazing, very few people can agree on how the recipe came about. "There are more stories about that recipe than there are leaves in a forest," says Mr. Smith. I decided to head to Harris Pass to see if I could figure out the truth about that recipe.

wouldn't emphasize the things about the town that I wanted to emphasize, and it wouldn't show the people's personality like it does now." I was particularly impressed by this student's awareness of the ways the hyperbolic language he uses in this piece impact it by emphasizing important information and conveying the townspeople's personalities.

Final Thoughts on Interpreting Figures of Speech and Understanding Their Roles in a Text

- ◆ Common Core Language Standard L.9–10.5.A emphasizes the importance of students understanding figures of speech—words and phrases used for effect that provide alternatives to straightforward expressions.
- ◆ Three especially important figures of speech for students to understand are euphemism, oxymoron, and hyperbole.
  - ◆ A euphemism is a figure of speech used to provide a gentler and more pleasant-sounding replacement for a statement that may feel harsh and offensive.
  - ◆ An oxymoron is the pairing of words or phrases that seem contradictory.
  - ◆ Hyperbole is a figure of speech in which a statement is intentionally exaggerated for impact.
- ◆ Figures of speech such as euphemism, oxymoron, and hyperbole allow authors to create pieces that align with their audiences and purposes as closely and effectively as possible. The specific benefits they provide are unique to their particular attributes:
  - ◆ Euphemism is an important tool for effective writing because it allows authors to use language throughout a work that is consistent with the piece's overall tone. For example, if a writer intends to use formal language throughout a piece of writing, she might employ euphemisms that have a formal-sounding tone to achieve this goal.
  - ◆ The figurative language strategy of oxymoron provides authors with the ability to add nuance and complexity to their works. The counterintuitive nature of oxymoron use allows writers to express intricate thoughts that more straightforward language may not allow.
  - ◆ Authors use the concept of hyperbole to provide extra emphasis to statements that are particularly significant. Through the use of hyperbole, authors can intentionally exaggerate a description of an event or action to call readers' attention to its importance
- ◆ When teaching students about the purposeful use of euphemism, oxymoron, and hyperbole:

- ◆ Show students published examples of euphemism, oxymoron, and hyperbole.
- ◆ Talk with students about how the published examples you've shown them are enhanced by the figures of speech they contain.
- ◆ Ask students to work collaboratively to find examples of these figures of speech and analyze their importance.
- ◆ Have students apply the strategies of euphemism, oxymoron, and hyperbole to their own works.
- ◆ Facilitate student reflection on the impact of these figures of speech on the pieces they create.

Section 2

Grammatical Concepts Aligned with Common Core
Language Standards for Grades 11 and 12

5

Vary Syntax for Effect

In this chapter, we'll look at the idea of varying syntax for effect, a strategy that requires authors to think carefully and purposefully about how and why they organize the grammatical concepts in the sentences they create. In the first section of this chapter, we'll explore what it means to vary syntax for effect and how writers achieve these variations in their works. Then, in the next section, we'll consider how varying syntax can be an important tool for effective writing. After that, we'll look inside an eleventh-grade classroom and check out how the students in that class work to understand this concept. Finally, I'll share five key recommendations to keep in mind when helping your students grasp this form of grammar use.

What Is It?

The strategy of varying syntax for effect refers to the choices authors make when organizing sentences in their works. When implementing this writing tool, authors consider the possible ways they'll structure their sentences and the impacts that those structural options can have on their readers. The Common Core State Standards emphasize the importance of this concept: Standard L.11–12.3 calls for students to "vary syntax for effect" (Core Standards, 2010). Grammar experts Don and Jenny Killgallon (2010) identify three key ways writers can vary the structure of sentences, all of which relate to way verbs are placed and organized in those sentences: single-verb sentences, multiple-verb sentences, and inverted-verb sentences. We'll examine each of these syntactical variations individually.

Figure 5.1 Key Information about Single-Verb, Multiple-Verb, and Inverted-Verb Sentences

Sentence Type	Description	Example
Single-Verb Sentence	Sentence structure containing one verb that is used to clearly and directly express a single action.	"The chef seasoned the fish perfectly."
Multiple-Verb Sentence	Sentence structure containing a series of verbs that are used to express a number of related actions.	"The chef sautéed the vegetables, grilled the steak, and simmered the sauce."
Inverted-Verb Sentence	Sentence structure that places the verb in the sentence before the subject.	"In the very back of the crowded dining room stood the smiling restaurant owner."

Single-Verb Sentences

Single-verb sentences contain one verb that is used to clearly and directly express a single action. The sentence "The chef seasoned the fish perfectly" is an example of a single-verb sentence; it uses one verb to convey a single action in a straightforward way.

Multiple-Verb Sentences

Multiple-verb sentences contain a series of verbs that are used to express a number of related actions. For example, the sentence "The chef sautéed the vegetables, grilled the steak, and simmered the sauce" uses a series of verbs to describe a number of tasks performed by the chef.

Inverted-Verb Sentences

Inverted-verb sentences take the traditional structure of English sentences and flip it around: while most sentences position the subject before the verb, inverted-verb sentences place the verb before the subject. Most inverted-verb sentences begin with some description information, which is followed by the verb and the subject. The sentence "In the very back of the crowded dining room stood the smiling restaurant owner" is an example of this sentence construction: it begins with the prepositional phrase "in the very back of the crowded dining room," which is followed by the verb "stood." The subject "the smiling restaurant owner" doesn't appear until the very end of the sentence. Figure 5.1 identifies the key attributes of each of these three sentence types.

Why Is This Concept Important to Effective Writing?

Varying syntax for effect is an important tool for effective writing because it allows authors to organize their sentences in ways that best correspond with the messages they want to convey. The three sentence structures we're exploring in this chapter—single-, multiple-, and inverted-verb sentences—all create different effects on a piece of writing and therefore all have individualized reasons for their importance. Since each one of these sentence types impacts a written work in a specific way, we'll look at the structures one at a time, analyzing published versions of each of them.

Why Are Single-Verb Sentences Important to Effective Writing?

Single-verb sentences are excellent writing tools to use when an author wants to express a single action clearly and directly. These sentences focus readers' attentions on a specific event, which is an especially useful tactic when an author wants to emphasize a particularly important action. In the 1940 novel *For Whom the Bell Tolls*, Ernest Hemingway uses a single-verb structure in the sentence "I will carry the pack" (p. 12). This sentence, which conveys a statement made by the book's protagonist Robert Jordan, expresses a single idea—in this case, that Jordan is willing to carry a pack of dynamite by himself. If this sentence expressed a number of actions, it wouldn't focus the readers' attention as directly on a single event. For example, if Hemingway had written, "I will carry the pack and read the map," there wouldn't be as much emphasis on Jordan carrying the backpack as there currently is.

Why Are Multiple-Verb Sentences Important to Effective Writing?

Multiple-verb sentences help writers keep their readers engaged for extended periods of time; the series of actions depicted in these sentences can pull readers in and keep their interests. In addition, these sentences can enhance the flow of a piece of writing by linking related thoughts and giving writers an alternative to shorter, choppier statements. Let's return to Hemingway's *For Whom the Bell Tolls* for an example of this sentence type: Hemingway describes Robert Jordan's actions toward a woman named Maria by saying, "He climbed down and took the bucket and helped her up the last boulder" (p. 323). In this sentence, Hemingway uses a multiple-verb structure to engage readers and maximize the sense of flow in the text. If the author did not choose to craft a multiple-verb sentence here, the language would be much choppier and less pleasant to read; rewritten as multiple single-verb sentences, this text could read, "Robert climbed down. He took the bucket. Then, he helped her up the last boulder." While single-verb sentences are effective in situations aligned with their features and structure, this particular sentence's impact is maximized by the multiple-verb syntax that Hemingway employs.

Why Are Inverted-Verb Sentences Important to Effective Writing?

Inverted-verb sentences provide authors with two key benefits: since they place the subject after the verb, sentences written in this way can vary sentence openings and create feelings of suspense. Sentences that use this structure can help authors vary the beginnings of sentences because they begin with descriptive details like prepositional phrases. If an author has begun a number of consecutive sentences with the same subject, she or he might want to use an inverted-verb structure that places the subject later in the sentence for some variety. Inverted-verb sentences can also create suspense, as they can cause readers to wait until later in the sentence to learn who performed an action or what is being described in the sentence. Hemingway uses this sentence type in *For Whom the Bell Tolls*: "On her face there was still a shadow of the expression the mention of the blinding had put there" (p. 223). This sentence describes a woman named Pilar's negative reaction to a conversation other characters in the book had about blinding a man named Pablo and selling him. The inverted-verb structure of this sentence provides variation to its beginning—the two preceding sentences in the book began with a noun or pronoun—and suspense, since we don't learn until about halfway through the sentence exactly what was on Pilar's face.

As these examples from *For Whom the Bell Tolls* indicate, the syntactical structures of single-verb, multiple-verb, and inverted-verb sentences are important writing tools that authors use strategically based on the kinds of effects they want to convey in their pieces. None of these options are inherently better or worse than another: the effectiveness of each sentence type depends on how closely it aligns with an author's goals. In the next section, we'll take a look inside an eleventh-grade classroom and examine how the students there explore the effectiveness of these sentence structures.

A Classroom Snapshot

"Today's the day," I tell the eleventh-grade class with which I'm working, "that you think about *Tess of the D'Urbervilles* totally differently."

As one might expect, this cryptic comment is met by a mixture of amused smiles and quizzical looks; noticing these reactions, I continue: "In today's class, we're going to do an activity that combines *Tess of the D'Urbervilles* [the novel, published by Thomas Hardy in 1891, that the class had just finished studying] with the ideas we've examined about single-verb, multiple-verb, and inverted-verb sentences. For this activity, you'll work in groups to find two of these syntactical structures in the book and comment on the importance of each sentence type you identify."

I place the chart depicted in Figure 5.2 on the document camera and explain its significance: "When you work on this activity, your group will complete this graphic organizer. As you'll notice, the organizer asks you to identify two different kinds of sentences from *Tess of the D'Urbervilles*: one that uses a single-verb, multiple-verb, or inverted-verb structure, and another that uses a different one of these types. For example, you might identify one single-verb sentence and one inverted-verb sentence, or any other combination of these three types—as long as you have two different kinds. Then, for each sentence, state which kind of structure it utilizes and explain why you think author Thomas Hardy chose to use that sentence type."

"When you work on this," I continue, "I want you to think carefully about why you think Hardy chose to use a particular sentence type in a specific situation: that's where you'll be doing some in-depth critical thinking. For example, did he use a single-verb sentence because he wanted to express one singular idea? Did he use a multiple-verb sentence to make a passage flow well and connect some related actions? Did he use an inverted-verb to build up some suspense and vary the beginning of a sentence?"

"Before you get started," I remark, "I want to show you a model of what this activity can look like. A sentence I noticed from *Tess of the D'Urbervilles* is on page 26 of the book: 'Mrs. Durbeyfield, having quickly walked hitherward after parting from Tess, opened the front door, crossed the downstairs room, which was in deep gloom, and then unfastened the stair-door like one whose fingers knew the tricks of the latches well.' If I used this sentence for the activity, I'd write it on the graphic organizer

Figure 5.2 Graphic Organizer for Syntax Analysis Activity

Sentence from the Text	Sentence Type (Single-Verb, Multiple-Verb, or Inverted-Verb)	Why You Think the Author Chose to Use This Sentence Type
1.		
2.		

in the first column. Then, I'd get to the second column, which asks me to identify the sentence type. I'd identify this excerpt as a multiple-verb sentence; there's definitely a series of verbs that convey a number of related actions: we learn in this sentence that Mrs. Durbeyfield opened a door, crossed a room, and unfastened another door. That's a lot of actions! The last column of the chart asks why the author may have chosen to use this sentence type—in this case, a multiple-verb sentence. I think Hardy chose to use this sentence type because he's discussing a number of related actions that logically move from one to the next. Since these actions are closely related and are all important, it works well to combine them into one sentence. If Mrs. Durbeyfield was only performing one action—or if one action was much more important than the others—then a single-verb sentence would work better. In this case, though, the multiple-verb sentence seems to best align with Hardy's purpose."

I tell the students that it's now their time to work on the activity; I give each group a copy of the graphic organizer and allow the students a few minutes to work before I check in with them. For a while, I move around the room and listen from a distance to the students' conversations. Once it seems like they are finishing up their work, I sit down with each of the groups and ask what they've noticed. I pull up a chair next to a group of students that looks to be finished; a group member explains to me that the first sentence from *Tess of the D'Urbervilles* they used for this activity was "Among these on-lookers were three young men of a superior class, carrying small knapsacks strapped to their shoulders, and stout sticks in their hands" (p. 16). Next I ask the students in this group to comment further: "Great job identifying this sentence," I tell them. "Now, let's talk about its type. What of our three syntactical structures do you think that sentence represents?"

"It's an inverted-verb sentence," replies a student. "It starts with 'among these on-lookers.' Then, it has the verb 'were.' Then after the verb is the subject, the part about the three young men of a superior class."

"Awesome!" I respond. "You did a really nice job of identifying this sentence type and noting its particular features. How about the last column on the chart that asks why you think the author chose to use this sentence type? Why do you think Hardy chose to use an inverted-verb sentence here?"

"Our group talked about how he did it to build up the suspense," responds a group member. "[Hardy] is writing about a dance and some of the people there. If he had said, 'Three young men of a superior class were among these onlookers,' there wouldn't really be any suspense—you wouldn't need to wait for anything—but with it as an inverted sentence, you have to wait to see who the author's actually talking about. It creates a lot more suspense."

"Fantastic work!" I exclaim. "I especially love how you compared the existing sentence construction with how the sentence would read if it was not an inverted-verb sentence. That's a really effective way to show the impact of the inverted-verb construction that Hardy uses. Great job!"

This group then shares with their insightful identification and analysis of another syntactical structure—this time, a multiple-verb sentence. I conclude my conversation with them and move around the rest of the classroom, speaking with all of the other student groups. At the end of the class meeting, I tell the students how proud I am of their work: "I'm so impressed by all of you. You did so well at finding and identifying examples from *Tess of the D'Urbervilles* of the sentence types we've discussed. In addition, and even more impressively, you gave outstanding explanations of why you think Hardy chose to use each sentence type. I told you at the beginning of class that you'd look at *Tess of the D'Urbervilles* totally differently in this activity. You did that, and you did it very well! Good work!"

Instructional Recommendations

This section details a step-by-step instructional process to use when helping students understand the grammatical concept of varying syntax for effect. The instructional steps I recommend are: 1) Show students published examples of single-verb, multiple-verb, and inverted-verb sentences; 2) Talk with students about why each of these sentence structures are important to effective writing; 3) Have students work together to identify and analyze these sentences types; 4) Confer with students as they apply these sentence structures to their own works; and 5) Help students reflect on the impacts these sentence types have on the pieces they create. Because these steps are intended to help students apply their knowledge of varying syntax for effect, I recommend using the descriptions and information at the beginning of this chapter, such as the chart depicted in Figure 5.1, to make sure students grasp the fundamental components of this concept before starting the instructional process.

1. Show students published examples of single-verb, multiple-verb, and inverted-verb sentences.

This initial step often enhances student "buy-in" to this grammatical concept; I've found students to be much more engaged in conversations about grammar when I've shown them published examples of a specific grammatical structure or idea. Presenting excerpts from a published text that embody the effective use of a key grammatical component has two major benefits: it develops students' understanding of a concept while also showing them its applicability. When I first thought about how I would present the grammatical concept of varying syntax for effect to an eleventh-grade class, I was worried that it would be difficult to get them to really get interested in this grammar tool. However, once I showed them the examples from *For Whom the Bell Tolls* described in this chapter, the students immediately sensed the relevance of the concept. Seeing how Hemingway applied single-verb, multiple-verb, and inverted-sentences to his work conveyed to students that these syntactical variations don't just exist in grammar workbooks and out-of-context activities: they're found in authentic examples of outstanding writers created by authors whose works are widely read and admired.

2. Talk with students about why each of these sentence structures is important to effective writing.

Once students have seen published examples of single-verb, multiple-verb, and inverted-verb, they'll be well-positioned to engage in a dialogue with you about the impact of each of these structures. To facilitate this conversation and analysis, I recommend asking students to consider the question "Why would an author do this?" regarding each of these sentence forms. For example, when talking with my students about the importance of multiple-verb sentences, I reminded them of the multiple-verb sentence from *For Whom the Bell Tolls* I showed them in the previous step: "Think back to the multiple-verb example we checked out recently, 'He climbed down and took the bucket and helped her up the last boulder' (p. 323). In this example, why do you think Hemingway chose to use a number of verbs in one sentence? Why not just make different sentences, each one with a different verb?"

As the students responded to these questions, I helped them understand that each sentence variation is a tool that writers use strategically, with a clear understanding of how it enhances the effectiveness of their piece. In the case of the Hemingway sentence we examined, our class discussion focused on the idea that linking these related actions together enhanced the readability of the piece and helped draw the reader into this narration. One student shared, "The sentence is a lot smoother with the multiple verbs than it would be if it just used one and was broken up into a bunch of shorter sentences. I think that's why Hemingway used this type of sentence here: he wanted it to be smooth and to sound good." This student's insights into the effectiveness of this multiple-verb sentence reveal his understanding of why Hemingway chose to use this syntactical structure in this scenario.

3. Have students work together to identify and analyze these sentences types.

This third step calls for students to take additional responsibility for their learning by working collaboratively to identify examples of sentence types, state which sentence type each identified example is, and comment on why they think the author of the piece chose to use each of these types. When working with your students on this activity, an example of which is described in the classroom snapshot, I recommend taking some key steps to facilitate the students' successes.

First, determine which book or books you'd like the students to use for the activity. In the classroom snapshot example, I asked students to identify examples from a book they recently read as a class, *Tess of the D'Urbervilles*. Asking students to use a book they've read as a whole class has some significant benefits, as it connects logically with other work they've done in English class and ensures that everyone in the class is familiar with the text being discussed. However, giving students the option of selecting a book they've used for independent reading also can work well, as it can provide additional flexibility and give students the opportunity to select from a high-interest text.

Once you've decided on the text or texts to be used, I recommend giving students a graphic organizer to help them structure their work on the activity. I like to use the organizer depicted in Figure 5.2 for this purpose, as it prompts students to find one of the relevant sentence structures, identify its type, and comment on why they believe the author chose to use that sentence form. In addition to providing students with this graphic organizer, I suggest modeling for students how to use it. For example, in the classroom snapshot, I explain how I showed my students how I filled out an entry on this graphic organizer using a selection from *Tess of the D'Urbervilles* before asking them to do the same.

When the students have a clear understanding of how to complete the activity, you can allow them to work in their groups on the task. Once the student groups appear close to finished, I like to talk with each group about their observations and analyses. A group of students in the class described in this chapter's snapshot identified the multiple-verb sentence "They entered upon the turf, and, impelled by an irresistible force, slackened their speed, stood still, turned, and waited beside the stone" (p. 397). A student in this group insightfully commented that "[Hardy] probably used this sentence type to connect these actions. Putting them all together in one sentence makes it like one long sequence instead of separate things." I like asking students to conduct these group analyses because of the experience the activity gives them in thinking about the impact of these syntactical structures.

4. Confer with students as they apply these sentence structures to their own works.

At this point in the instructional process, I ask students to use the syntactical forms we've been discussing in their own pieces. When we reach this stage in this process, I tell my students that I feel they're ready to take increased ownership of their work and that I'm confident in their abilities to apply the concept of varying syntax for effect. "You've shown me that you know this information," I recently told my eleventh graders, "by identifying single-verb, multiple-verb, and inverted-verb sentences and thinking carefully about why authors use each of these types in specific instances. Now, for the next step: using one or more of these sentence types in your writing!" Before asking my students to get started, I do two things. First, I review the features of these sentence types and the reasons why authors use them. Second, I remind them of the purpose of using these sentence types purposefully. "I don't want you to just use some of these sentence types for the sake of using them," I explained to my students. "Instead, I want you to think about which sentence types are the best ways to express what you want to say. If you don't feel an inverted-verb sentence, for example, is the best way to express anything you want to say, then don't use that sentence type. It's up to you whether you use one, two, or three of these sentence types; just make sure the ones you use align with whatever you are saying."

While the students work on purposefully integrating these syntactical structures into their pieces, I suggest holding one-on-one conferences with them that focus on how they're doing. In these conferences, I like to ask students to identify an example of one of these sentence types and explain why they think that structure is the best one to use in that context. I recently met with a student who was crafting a personal narrative about his experience playing baseball in the State Tournament. In our conference, he identified an example of a single-verb and one of a multiple-verb sentence, explaining that each sentence type best aligned with what he was trying to say: "When I was talking about catching the ball at the end of the game, I used a single-verb sentence. It's one action, so a single-verb sentence was the best way to write about it, but earlier, when I was writing about running from second base all the way to home and then sliding past the catcher's tag, I used a multiple-verb sentence. I was talking about a bunch of related actions, so I figured a multiple-verb sentence was the best one to use." The student's comments reveal his understanding of how these sentence types are best used if they are carefully selected based on the information that the author wants to convey.

5.   Help students reflect on the impacts these sentence types have on the pieces they create.

Concluding this instructional process by asking students to consider how the sentence types they used impacted their works causes them to think metacognitively about the syntactical variations they've studied and applied, helping them develop deep understandings of the significance of this grammar tool. To facilitate the students' reflections, I like to ask them a series of related questions that call for them to think critically about one of the sentence types they used in their works and its impact on the piece: 1) What is one of the sentence structures we've discussed that you used in your writing?; 2) Identify an example of that structure. How did your use of it enhance your piece?; and 3) How would your piece be different if you had used a different sentence structure instead?

The previously-described student who used a number of these sentence types when discussing his experiences playing baseball explained that a multiple-verb in his narrative enhanced the quality of his writing: "It makes the story I'm telling fast-paced. It's about related actions that happened quickly and putting it all in one sentence tells about the actions in a fast-paced way that is like how it all really went down." He continued to note how this section of his piece would be different if he had used another sentence structure: "The [other sentence structures] wouldn't be as fast-paced as the multiple-verb one is because the multiple-verb sentence emphasizes the related actions. The single-verb one would make the actions seem more separate, and the inverted-verb one would build suspense about who was doing the action, which wasn't really what I was trying to do here."

After this student shared his reflections, I told him that I was very happy that he was looking at the relationship between each sentence type and how it aligns with the kind of information he wanted to convey. "That's what really good writers do," I explained. "They know the best sentence type, grammatical concept, or writing strategy to use is the one that best fits with what they want to say."

Final Thoughts on Varying Syntax for Effect

- ◆ Common Core State Standard L.11–12.3 calls for students to "vary syntax for effect" (Core Standards, 2010).
- ◆ Grammar experts Don and Jenny Killgallon (2010) identify three key ways writers can vary the structure of sentences: single-verb sentences, multiple-verb sentences, and inverted-verb sentences.
  - ◆ A single-verb sentence contains one verb and is used to clearly and directly express a single action.
  - ◆ A multiple-verb sentence contains a series of verbs and is used to express a number of related actions.
  - ◆ An inverted-verb sentence places the verb in the sentence before the subject.
- ◆ Each of these syntactical variations enhances a piece of writing in a way that is unique to its characteristics.
  - ◆ Single-verb sentences are excellent writing tools to use when an author wants to express a single action clearly and directly. These sentences focus readers' attentions on a

specific event, which is an especially useful tactic when an author wants to emphasize a particularly important action.

◆ Multiple-verb sentences help writers keep their readers engaged for extended periods of time; the series of actions depicted in these sentences can pull readers in and keep their interests. In addition, these sentences can enhance the flow of a piece of writing by linking related thoughts and giving writers an alternative to shorter, choppier statements.

◆ Inverted-verb sentences provide authors with two key benefits: since they place the subject after the verb, sentences written in this way can vary sentence openings and create feelings of suspense. Sentences that use this structure can help authors vary the beginnings of sentences because they begin with descriptive details like prepositional phrases. Inverted-verb sentences can create suspense by causing readers to wait until later in the sentence to learn who performed an action or what is being described in the sentence.

◆ When teaching students about the writing strategy of varying syntax for effect:

  ◆ Show students published examples of single-verb, multiple-verb, and inverted-verb sentences.

  ◆ Talk with students about why each of these sentence structures are important to effective writing.

  ◆ Have students work together to identify and analyze these sentences types.

  ◆ Confer with students as they apply these sentence structures to their own works.

  ◆ Help students reflect on the impacts these sentence types have on the pieces they create.

6

Analyze Nuances in the Meanings of Words with Similar Denotations

This chapter describes an important aspect of grammatical and linguistic knowledge: analyzing and understanding nuanced differences in the meanings of words with similar denotations. First, we'll explore what it means to analyze nuances in the meanings of words with similar denotations. Then, we'll consider why awareness of this concept is important to effective writing. Next, we'll examine what a lesson on this topic can look like. Finally, we'll look at key recommendations to keep in mind when helping your students understand and apply this concept.

What Is It?

One reason effective communication is so complex is that authors need to consider both the denotations and the connotations of the words they use. The Common Core Language Standards emphasize the importance of understanding the nuanced connotations of words with similar denotations: Standard L.11–12.5.B calls for students to consider this concept. To fully understand this concept, let's explore what denotations and connotations are.

Denotation
A word's denotation is its dictionary definition, which captures its basic meaning. For example, the adjectives "old" and "vintage" have very similar denotations when used to describe an object: both characterize an item as being from an earlier time period. However, one would not typically use these two words interchangeably; to understand why, we need to consider the connotation attached to each word.

Connotation

A word's connotation is its associative meaning, or the feelings and emotions that correspond with the word. Often, words with similar denotations have different connotations; for example, the previously-mentioned words "old" and "vintage" connote different feelings and attitudes. "Old" typically carries a negative connotation, while "vintage" is often associated with a positive one. A description of "an old car" would likely not be used to send a positive message about that car to a reader, but a discussion of a "vintage" one probably would. Figure 6.1 depicts key ideas related to meanings of denotation and connotation.

Why Is This Concept Important to Effective Writing?

Understanding and analyzing nuanced connotative differences in words with similar denotations is a key component to effective writing: it enables authors to clearly communicate information with their audiences and to ensure that their statements are understood as they originally intended. To illustrate the importance of this concept, let's imagine what might take place if an author didn't think carefully about nuanced differences in words with similar denotations. Chinua Achebe's 1959 book *Things Fall Apart* describes the accomplishments of Okonkwo, the novel's protagonist, stating, "As a young man of eighteen he had brought honor to his village…" (p. 4). If Achebe had used a word with a similar denotative meaning to "honor" but a different connotative one, the passage would have a different tone. For example, if he used "attention" instead, the text would read, "As a young man of eighteen he had brought attention to his village…" While both "honor" and "attention" have similar

Figure 6.1 Key Ideas Related to Denotation and Connotation

Term	Definition	Explanation
Denotation	The dictionary definition of a word.	The adjectives "old" and "vintage" have similar denotations: they can both be used to characterize an item as being from an earlier time period.
Connotation	The associative meaning of a word (the feelings or emotions that correspond with it).	The adjectives "old" and "vintage" have different connotations: "old" typically carries a negative connotation, while "vintage" is often associated with a positive one.

denotations as they're used here, "honor" has a much more positive connotation than "attention," which doesn't have the same positive association. Even if Achebe had used another word with a positive connotation, it might not have as strong of an emotion connected to it as "honor" does. For example, if he used the word "recognition" to form the passage, "As a young man of eighteen he had brought recognition to his village…", the revised text would not convey the same level of positivity as the original one.

The importance of this concept is again represented in another passage from *Things Fall Apart:* when describing a woman named Anasi, Chinua Achebe explains, "There was authority in her bearing and she looked every inch the ruler of the womenfolk in a large and prosperous family" (p. 20). Achebe's use of the word "authority," which illustrates Anasi's strong presence and appearance, exemplifies the significance of writers considering the nuanced differences of words with similar denotations. If he had instead used "dominance," which has a similar denotative meaning in this case to "authority," the sentence would have a more aggressive tone than it currently does. The statement "There was dominance in her bearing…" suggests a forceful figure who treats others harshly; "authority," on the other hand, suggests someone who is respected and powerful, but is not associated with violence or aggression.

The writing strategy of analyzing nuanced differences in words with similar denotations is essential to clear and successful communication. If a writer didn't keep this concept in mind, his or her work could suffer: there may be a misalignment between what the author wants to say and what readers think he or she is saying. It would be very confusing if a writer wanted to deliver a positive message about something, but instead used an adjective with a negative connotation to describe it (such as the "vintage" and "old" examples discussed earlier in this chapter). In the next section, we'll take a look inside an eleventh-grade class and examine how those students work to understand this concept.

A Classroom Snapshot

My eleventh graders have been doing a great job analyzing the differences in meaning of words with similar denotations, so I decide to open today's class by telling them so. However, I think it would be especially fun to praise them with also making a connection to this grammatical and linguistic concept; with this in mind, I direct two statements to my students at the beginning of this morning's class: "Your recent insights on connotation and denotation have been splendorous!" and "Your recent insights on connotation and denotation have been on fleek!" After making these statements, I ask the students, "Who can tell me how those comments relate to our conversations about connotation and denotation?"

"I know," replies a laughing student seated in the front of the room. "They have the same denotations but the connotations are different. Nice job using 'on fleek,' by the way, Dr. R."

"Thanks," I respond, smiling, glad that my attempt to use contemporary language has amused the students. "Like you said, these two adjectives have similar denotations, but different connotations. Even though both 'splendorous' and 'on fleek' are associated with positive things, their connotations are different because 'splendorous' is associated with a formal and old-fashioned tone, while 'on fleek' has a more current and informal feeling to it."

Today is the third class meeting devoted to analyzing nuanced connotative differences in words with similar denotations that I've had with these students. In our first session, we discussed the meanings of connotation and denotation and looked together at examples of words that have similar denotative meanings but different connotative ones. Then, in our second class on the topic, we explored the importance of this concept to effective writing: to do so, we considered how the meanings of published sentences (such as the excerpts from *Things Fall Apart* described earlier in this chapter) would be different if certain words in those sentences were replaced with others that had similar denotations but different connotations. In today's class, we'll get more interactive: I'll ask the students to work in groups to select sentences from published texts, replace a word in that sentence with one that has a similar denotation but different connotation, and analyze how the meaning of the revised sentence differs from the original one.

After I discuss these directions with the students, I give each small group of students the handout depicted in Figure 6.2. (A reproducible version of this graphic organizer is depicted in Appendix B.)

Once each group has a copy of the document, I describe its contents: "Here's the graphic organizer for you to use as you work on this activity. It asks for you to identify a sentence from the text, decide on a word you'd like to replace, decide on another word with a similar denotation but different connotation, write a revised version of the sentence that contains the new word, and finally to analyze how the meaning of the new sentence differs from the original one."

I continue, explaining, "Before you all work on this activity in your groups, I'm going to model an example for you. Like all of you will do when you complete this activity, I'll start by identifying a sentence from a published text that I think would work for this assignment. The sentence I've found that I'd like to use is from the book *Winesburg, Ohio* by Sherwood Anderson (1919). It reads, 'Enoch Robinson sprang to his feet and ran to the window that looked down into the deserted main street of Winesburg' (p. 177). I decided to replace the word 'deserted' with a different word that has a similar denotation but a different connotation: I'm going to replace it with 'unoccupied.' With this replacement, the new

Figure 6.2 Graphic Organizer for Student Analysis of Connotation and Denotation

Original Excerpt	Word You Chose to Replace	Replacement Word with Similar Denotation but Different Connotation	New Version of Sentence	How the Meaning of the New Sentence Differs from the Original One

sentence is 'Enoch Robinson sprang to his feet and ran to the window that looked down into the unoccupied main street of Winesburg.' Now I'm going to think about how the meanings of the two sentences differ: both 'deserted' and 'unoccupied' indicate that the street is empty, but 'deserted' has a more negative connotation than 'unoccupied' does. Even though both words mean empty, 'deserted' suggests that the street has been completely vacated for a while and isn't a very desirable place to be, while 'unoccupied' suggests that the street is just empty right now. Think about these words in a different sentence: if I said, 'I walked into the deserted room,' you'd probably have more of a negative feeling about the room than if I said, 'I walked into the unoccupied room.' 'Unoccupied' just sounds like the room is currently empty; 'deserted' makes it sound like this room is a place where no one wants to be."

I continue, emphasizing the importance of connotation in these sentences: "By changing a word in this sentence from *Winesburg, Ohio* to another word with a different connotation, I altered the mood of the sentence, taking it from its original negative tone to a less-negative one. Now, I'm going to ask you and your group members to do the same work with another sentence from a book of your choice. You can select a book from our classroom library, use one you've already read this year, or utilize the book you're using for independent reading. Take some time to talk with your group members and get started on this activity; once some time has passed, I'll check in with each group and ask what you've found."

I move around the classroom, listening to the groups' analyses and conversations. Once a group appears to be finished, I sit down with them and ask about their work: "How did it go?" I inquire.

"We used *Song of Solomon* (Morrison, 1977) and found a good example," replies a student.

"Awesome," I respond. "Tell me what you found."

"The original excerpt from the book," answers a student in the group, "is 'Everyone knew the girls had spent hour after hour tracing, cutting, and stitching the costly velvet, and that Gerhardt's Department Store would be quick to reject any that were soiled'" (p. 5).

"And what word did you choose to replace?" I prompt the group members.

"We picked 'costly' and replaced it with 'precious,'" explains a student. "The new version of the sentence is 'Everyone knew the girls had spent hour after hour tracing, cutting, and stitching the precious velvet, and that Gerhardt's Department Store would be quick to reject any that were soiled.'"

"Wonderful!" I exclaim. "Now, tell me how the meaning of the new sentence differs from the original one."

"We said the new sentence is different because 'costly' and 'precious' have different connotations," states a group member. "In the original sentence, the one with 'costly' in it, the sentence is saying that the velvet costs a lot of money. In the second sentence, though, 'precious' gives it a different kind of meaning. 'Precious' has a stronger connotation. Something precious isn't just expensive. It also has the connotation of being valuable for another reason, like it's really rare or it's one of a kind."

"Really nice work, y'all," I praise the group members. "I love how thoughtfully you analyzed the differences in the connotations between the original word from the text, 'costly,' and your replacement word, 'precious.' You showed an awesome understanding of the differences in the connotations of these words. Very nicely done."

I continue to move around the classroom, similarly impressed by other groups' analyses of the connotations of specific words in the sentences they identified and their insights into how the meanings of those sentences would be different if the identified word was replaced with another that possesses a similar denotation but different connotation. I conclude the class meeting by commending the students' works and previewing what we'll be doing the next day: "Excellent work, today, all of you. I'm so happy with your strong understandings of how words with similar denotations but different connotations can alter the meanings and tones of sentences. Tomorrow, we'll talk about how to put this grammar tool into action in your own writings. I'm looking forward to talking with you about that!"

Instructional Recommendations

This section describes a step-by-step instructional process to follow when helping students understand how to analyze nuanced connotative differences in the meanings of words with similar denotations. The instructional steps I recommend are: 1) Show students published excerpts that contain words with specific connotations and explain those connotations; 2) Discuss how those excerpts would differ if they contained words with similar denotations but different connotations; 3) Ask students to work together to select published passages and analyze the importance of connotation in the meanings of those passages; 4) Work with students as they apply their understandings of connotation and denotation to their own writings; and 5) Have students reflect on how understanding this concept impacted the works they created. These steps are designed to help students apply their understandings of connotation and denotation, so I recommend using the examples and information discussed in the beginning of this chapter (such as the facts and explanations in Figure 6.1) to ensure students understand the fundamental components of this concept before beginning the instructional process.

1. Show students published excerpts that contain words with specific connotations and explain those connotations.

This initial step of the instructional process helps students see how the concepts of connotation and denotations are used authentically in writing. When recently doing this with my eleventh graders, I showed them the examples from *Things Fall Apart* described earlier in the chapter and identified words that I felt had particularly noteworthy connotations—that is, words that could be replaced by others that have similar denotative meanings but different connotative ones. For example, when I shared the excerpt "As a young man of eighteen he had brought honor to his village…" from *Things Fall Apart* with my students, I identified the word "honor" and discussed its connotation, noting, "The word 'honor' has a really positive feeling attached to it; by using this word, Achebe communicates to us that the kind of attention the character Okonkwo brought to his village was extremely positive." Similarly, when I shared the passage "There was authority in her bearing and she looked every inch the ruler of the womenfolk in a large and prosperous family," explaining that the word "authority" stands out to me because of its connotation: "In this sentence," I explained, "the word 'authority' has a specific connotation; it connotes power and respect. Some words that are associated with power aren't also associated with respect, but this one is."

To further develop my students' understandings of connotation, I also showed them two examples from *Moby Dick* (Melville, 1851) that contain language with specific connotations. First, I shared a statement by Ishmael, the novel's narrator, imagining his future experiences with sea captains: "Well, then, however the old sea-captains may order me about…" (p. 5). In this sentence, the word "old" suggests an irreverent tone; its use here doesn't connote a great deal of respect. Next, I shared a sentence in which Ishmael is describing the features of a chapel dedicated to whalers, focusing specifically on the attributes of the chapel's pulpit: "But the side ladder was not the only strange feature of the place, borrowed from the chaplain's former sea-farings" (p. 56). I explained to the students that the word "strange" carries a specific connotation: "Ishmael's talking about unusual attributes of the chapel," I told them, "and uses the word 'strange' to show his confusion about what he's noticing. There are words that have this same denotation but also have connotations with more positive messages. The use of 'strange' sends a message about Ishmael's confusion about this chapel and possibly about other aspects of the situation in which he finds himself."

2. Discuss how those excerpts would differ if they contained words with similar denotations but different connotations.

This instructional step helps students think in more depth about the importance of carefully considering the connotations of words with similar denotations. To engage students in this thoughtful analysis, I suggest taking the passages you used in the first step of this instructional process, replacing the key words you identified with others that have similar denotative meanings but different connotative ones, and discussing with your students the how the new language differs from the original. As mentioned earlier in this chapter, the meanings of the two excerpts I shared from *Things Fall Apart* change significantly if key words are changed to others with different connotations but similar denotations: changing "honor" to "recognition" in the first excerpt takes away some of the positive connotation in the original text, and replacing "authority" with "dominance" makes the sentence's tone more aggressive than respectful.

Similarly, when discussing the previously-described selections from *Moby Dick* with my students, I replaced the word "old" in the excerpt "Well, then, however the old sea-captains may order me about…" (p. 5) with "veteran." I then talked with my students about how the new text differs from the original version: "When we replace 'old' with 'veteran,' we get a new passage that says, 'Well, then, however the veteran sea-captains may order me about…'" I continued to comment on the impact of the new word: "This new version has a much more positive tone than the original one; 'old' has a slightly more negative connotation, while 'veteran' is more positive and respectful. If you wanted to describe someone in a positive way and you were choosing between these words, you'd likely use 'veteran' to show that you think highly of that person."

After discussing this example, I turned the students' attention to the other selection from *Moby Dick* we'd discussed: "But the side ladder was not the only strange feature of the place, borrowed from the chaplain's former sea-farings" (p. 56). In this conversation, I replaced the "strange" with "unique," a word with a similar denotative meaning but a different connotative one. This time, instead of sharing my thoughts on the difference with the students, I ask them to share their insights: "What do you all think about the differences in tone between these sentences? The original is 'But the side ladder was not the only strange feature of the place, borrowed from the chaplain's former sea-farings' and the new version is 'But the side ladder was not the only unique feature of the place, borrowed from the chaplain's former sea-farings.'"

"The new one sounds much better, much nicer," explains a student, "because 'unique' sounds like a nicer thing to say about something or someone than 'strange'."

"A great point!" I reply. "Let's discuss this further. Those two words have similar denotations—they both can mean something that's unlike others and different from what's typical—but they have different connotations. How do you all think the connotations of 'strange' and 'unique' are different?"

"'Strange' doesn't sound like a compliment, but 'unique' does. [Unique] has a much better and more positive connotation than 'strange.' 'Strange' is worse; it's more of a negative connotation."

"Excellent response!" I say, praising the student's insights.

When conducting this activity with your students, I recommend structuring it as I did when analyzing these examples from *Moby Dick* with my students: first modeling an example of an analysis for them and then asking them to analyze another excerpt using the same structure. When you're satisfied with your students' understandings and analyses, you can move to the next step of this instructional process!

3. Ask students to work together to select published passages and analyze the importance of connotation in the meanings of those passages.

This third step resembles the work done in the second instructional recommendation, but with one key difference: in this activity, more ownership is placed on the students—they work in groups to select a passage from a published text of their choice, choose a key word to replace, rewrite the sentence with another word that has a similar denotation but different connotation, and analyze the differences in the two sentences. (An example of this activity is described in this chapter's classroom snapshot.) Before asking the students to complete the activity, I recommend giving them the graphic organizer depicted in Figure 6.2 and modeling an example to give students clear understandings of what they're being asked to. For instance, in the instructional example described in the classroom snapshot, I modeled my own analysis of an excerpt from *Winesburg, Ohio* before asking the students to select a text and conduct their own analytical work.

In the snapshot, I discuss the insights of a group of students who used *Song of Solomon* for this activity. Another group in that class analyzed a section of Dave Eggers' (2009) book *Zeitoun,* selecting a sentence describing some of the main character's employees: "Other workers were just young men: irresponsible and living for today" (p. 19). This group then replaced the word "irresponsible" with "carefree," creating the sentence "Other workers were just young men: carefree and living for today." When I asked these students how the meaning of the new sentence differs from the original version, they had a number of insightful comments. One explained, "The new sentence sounds a lot kinder than the original. 'Carefree' sounds kind—it almost even sounds like a compliment. 'Irresponsible' doesn't sound very kind at all. It definitely sounds like an insult." Another student in the group noted, "It's kind of crazy how much of a difference connotation makes; even though these words have really similar meanings, their different connotations make the sentences so different!"

4. Work with students as they apply their understandings of connotation and denotation to their own writings.

Now that you've led your students through a number of discussions and analyses of connotation and denotation, I recommend giving them even more ownership by asking them to apply their understandings of this strategy to pieces of writing they're creating. I tell my students to do two things when putting their knowledge of connotation and denotation into action when they write: 1) Read what you've written, paying attention to the connotation of the words you use and making any necessary changes so that the connotation of the language in your piece aligns with your intended meaning; and 2) Keep the concepts of connotation and denotation in mind as you continue to write, focusing on ensuring that the connotative meanings of the words you chose correspond with the message you intend to send. Each of these steps is intended to help students see the connotation as a powerful tool that can help writers align the language they use with their intended messages.

As students apply their understandings of the nuances of connotation to their pieces, I recommend holding one-on-one conferences with them to monitor their progress and provide any needed support. When conferring with students about this topic, I like to ask them to identify a word they've used that has a specific connotation and then explain how that word's connotation aligns with the meaning and tone of the context in which it's used. This requires students to show how the connotations of the language they choose impacts their writings. In a recent conference about this topic, a student explained how he revised the first draft of his research paper on William Faulkner with connotation and denotation in mind: "In my first draft, I said that a building in New Orleans where Faulkner lived when he was getting started as a writer is now a small bookstore, but I changed 'small' to 'cozy' to give the description of the bookstore a more positive connotation."

5. Have students reflect on how understanding this concept impacted the works they created.

I concluded this instructional process by asking students to reflect on the importance of understanding the connotative differences between words with similar denotations which requires them to think carefully and analytically about the importance of this concept to effective writing. To facilitate these reflections, I recommend asking students to respond to two related questions about the impact of connotation on effective writing: 1) How did thinking about the different connotations of words with similar denotations make a positive impact on your writing?; and 2) How would your writing be impacted if you didn't consider this concept?

I asked the student whose work on William Faulkner is discussed in the previous recommendation to answer these questions; in response to the first one, he explained, "I think it made a positive impact on my writing because thinking about connotation helped me be sure to use a word that goes with the tone I'm trying to have. If I'm trying to have a positive, happy tone about something, it's important that I use words that have those kinds of connotations." The student then reacted to the second reflection question, saying, "My writing could be impacted a lot if I didn't think about connotation because I could accidentally use a word with a negative connotation when I'm trying to say something positive. This could be really confusing to the reader." This student's comments reveal his ability to think metacognitively about how an understanding of connotation can maximize the effectiveness of a piece of writing.

Final Thoughts on Analyzing Nuances in the Meanings of Words with Similar Denotations

- ◆ Common Core Language Standard L.11–12.5.B calls for students to understand the nuanced connotations of words with similar denotations.
- ◆ A word's denotation is its dictionary definition, which captures its basic meaning.
- ◆ A word's connotation is its associative meaning, or the feelings and emotions that correspond with the word.

◆ Often, words with similar denotations have different connotations; for example, the words "old" and "vintage" have similar denotations, but connote different feelings and attitudes.

◆ The writing strategy of analyzing nuanced differences in words with similar denotations is essential to clear and successful communication; it would be very confusing if a writer wanted to deliver a positive message about something, but instead used an adjective with a negative connotation to describe it.

◆ When teaching students how to analyze nuanced connotative differences in the meanings of words with similar denotations:

  ◆ Show students published excerpts that contain words with specific connotations and explain those connotations.

  ◆ Discuss how those excerpts would differ if they contained words with similar denotations but different connotations.

  ◆ Ask students to work together to select published passages and analyze the importance of connotation to the meanings of those passages.

  ◆ Work with students as they apply their understandings of connotation and denotation to their own writings.

  ◆ Have students reflect on how understanding this concept impacted the works they created.

7

Use Domain-Specific Words and Phrases

In this chapter, we'll examine the idea of using domain-specific words and phrases to enhance the quality of writing. To explore this strategy, we'll first discuss what it means to use domain-specific words and phrases. Then, we'll consider how this concept is important to effective writing. After that, we'll take a look inside a twelfth-grade class and see how those students work to understand this strategy. Finally, we'll check out five key recommendations to use when teaching students about domain-specific words and phrases.

What Is It?

The term "domain-specific words and phrases" refers to concrete and precise language that authors use to clearly and concretely express ideas and communicate information. This concept is applicable to all genres: writers of narrative, argument, and informational works must use specific language relevant to their domains and topics so that their readers can understand what they are trying to express. The Common Core Language Standards emphasize the importance of domain-specific words and phrases: Standard L.11–12.6 calls for students to understand and use this concept "at the college and career readiness level" (Core Standards, 2010). While we can't predict every topic our students will encounter in their colleges and careers, we can use the grammatical concepts of specific nouns and strong verbs to help students learn how to use specific language. Mastering these grammatical strategies will help them communicate in concrete and specific ways that are relevant to all the domains and topics they'll encounter and all the genres in which they'll need to write.

Specific Nouns

Specific nouns clearly and directly communicate particular people, places, things, or ideas. General nouns, on the other hand, refer to people, places, things, or ideas in broad and nonspecific ways. For example, the term "football helmet" is a specific noun, while "sports equipment" is a more general and nonspecific way to describe it. When recently discussing specific nouns with high school seniors, I found it useful to make connections to the different forms of technology they use. In one conversation on this topic, I explained that the students use specific nouns frequently when discussing the names of particular social media apps: "I hear you use a lot of specific nouns when you say things like 'I follow him on Instagram' or 'I saw her picture on Snapchat.' If you couldn't use specific nouns, you'd have to say things like 'I follow him on a social media app,' instead of 'Instagram.' This new version wouldn't be as informative and concrete." Figure 7.1 summarizes the definition of specific nouns and lists examples of specific and general nouns.

Strong Verbs

Strong verbs indicate the exact ways particular actions are performed. Weak verbs, on the other hand, are vague and don't clearly communicate the way actions are done. For example, in the sentence "I devoured the birthday cake," the strong verb "devoured" provides specific information about the way the speaker consumed the cake. By contrast, the sentence "I ate the cake" uses the weaker verb "ate," which doesn't clearly express how the action took place. Just as I did with specific nouns, I made connections to students' interests in technology when

Figure 7.1 Key Information about Specific Nouns

What Are Specific Nouns?	Specific nouns are terms that clearly and directly communicate a particular person, place, thing, or idea.
What Are Some Examples of Specific Nouns?	The players put on their **football helmets** before taking the field. ("Football helmets" is a specific noun in this sentence; "sports equipment" is a general noun that could be used instead.) I saw her picture on **Snapchat**. ("Snapchat" is a specific noun in this sentence; "a social media app" is a general noun version.)

Figure 7.2 Key Information about Strong Verbs

What Are Strong Verbs?	Strong verbs are words that indicate the exact way a particular action is performed.
What Are Some Examples of Strong Verbs?	I **devoured** the birthday cake. ("Devoured" is a strong verb in this sentence; "ate" is a weaker verb that could replace it.)
	I **texted** her the name of the restaurant where we're meeting. ("Texted" is a strong verb in this example; "sent" is a weaker, less-specific version.)

discussing the concept of strong verbs with them: "You use strong verbs a lot when you talk about communicating using technological devices," I explained. "You might say, 'I texted her the name of the restaurant where we're meeting' or 'I emailed my teacher with a question about the paper.' In these sentences, 'texted' and 'emailed' are strong verbs; if you used the weak verb 'sent' instead of these strong versions, you wouldn't know how the information was communicated. With the strong verbs, you know exactly how the subject shared the information." Figure 7.2 includes the definition of strong verbs, as well as examples of strong and weak verbs.

Why Is This Concept Important to Effective Writing?

Domain-specific language is essential to effective writing because it allows authors and their readers to have the same understandings of key information. No matter the genre in which an author is writing, it's critical for writers to communicate ideas to their audiences in the exact ways they want those ideas to be understood. I recently explained this point to my students, highlighting the fact that domain-specific language is central to all kinds of writing: "Whether you're writing a story, or an informational report, or an argumentative piece, your writing needs clear and specific language for it to be effective. If I'm writing a fictional narrative and I use vague, general nouns, you won't know exactly what I'm trying to describe. If I want to say that the characters in the story approached a shack and I use the word 'building' to say what they approached, my readers won't have a clear understanding of what I'm talking about. There are tons of different types of buildings readers could picture, so we probably wouldn't have the same understanding of the information. However, if I used the specific noun 'shack,' my readers and I would be on the same page in terms of what's going on in the story." In the remainder of this section, we'll consider specific nouns and strong verbs individually, reflecting on why each of these forms of domain-specific language is essential to effective writing and looking at published examples to convey the importance of each one.

Why Are Specific Nouns Important to Effective Writing?

As the "shack" example I shared with my students illustrates, specific nouns are important tools for effective writing because they allow for readers and writers to have shared understandings of the same people, places, things, and ideas. A great way to illustrate the impact of this concept is by looking at examples of it in multiple genres. In Bill Bryson's (2003) nonfiction text *A Short History of Nearly Everything*, the author uses the specific noun "astronomers" to provide clarity to the statement "A few astronomers continue to think there may yet be a Planet X out there—a real whopper, perhaps as much as ten times the size of Jupiter, but so far out as to be invisible to us" (p. 29). If Bryson had used a more general noun such as "people" in place of "astronomers," we readers wouldn't have a clear understanding of the information he is trying to communicate. We might ask ourselves questions like "Who are these people?" and "What are their qualifications?" Even if Bryson had used the noun "scientists," which is more specific than "people" but still not as concrete as "astronomers," the sentence wouldn't be as clear as its original version is: we wouldn't know what kinds of scientists they are or what they study. The specific noun "astronomers" allows readers to comprehend the writer's message in detail.

Now, let's turn our attention to the use of this strategy in fiction. The narrator of the novel *Invisible Man* (Ellison, 1947) describes a man with whom he had an altercation, saying, "He lay there, moaning on the asphalt…" (p. 5). In this excerpt, the specific noun "asphalt" ensures that the narrator clearly communicates the kind of surface on which the man lay moaning. If the text said the man was "on the ground," readers would have a general idea of where he was, but the piece would lack the specific detail that the current version has. We readers wouldn't know what kind of ground it is, and therefore would have a difficult time picturing the situation. In contrast, the precise usage of the noun "asphalt" clearly communicates the specifics of the situation to us readers, making it easy for us to visualize the scenario as the narrator intends it.

Why Are Strong Verbs Important to Effective Writing?

Strong verbs are important to effective writing because they communicate how actions are performed and provide insights into the feelings and moods surrounding those actions. When recently discussing the importance of this concept with my students, I explained how strong verbs achieve both of these objectives: "When you use a strong verb, you let your reader know exactly what an action looked like, but you can also do even more: you can give your information about how the performer of that action feels about it. For example, let's say you're writing an article for the school newspaper about a soccer game. If you said, 'Before the game, the players dashed onto the field,' you'd use the strong verb 'dashed' to express the exact way the team performed this action and to convey information about the players' feelings. Since dashing is a very fast way to move readers can infer that the players were probably excited to get on the field so the game could start. If you wrote, 'Before the game, the players went onto the field,' you'd still communicate the same basic action, but the weak verb 'went' would really change the sentence for your readers. Since the readers wouldn't know exactly how the action was performed, they wouldn't be able to picture how the players went onto the field or infer anything about those players' emotions."

In *A Short History of Nearly Everything*, Bill Bryson uses the strong verb "examined" to clearly describe the treatment of a set of mastodon bones, stating, "In 1795 a selection of bones made their way to Paris, where they were examined by the rising star of paleontology, the youthful and aristocratic Georges Cuvier" (p. 105). The author's use of this verb allows readers to form a concrete image of Cuvier examining the bones; if Bryson had written that the bones were to be "seen" or "looked at," readers wouldn't have the same clear understanding of *how* Cuvier performed this action. We'd know that the paleontologist saw the bones, but wouldn't have the clear understanding that "examined" provides. In addition, the strong verb provides information about the mood surrounding Georges Cuvier's interaction with the mastodon bones, as it suggests a serious and intense mood. Weaker verbs like "seen" and "looked at" would not imply these same emotions.

Ralph Ellison's narrator uses the strong verb "lunged" in *Invisible Man*, saying, "I lunged for a yellow coin lying on the blue design of the carpet..." (p. 27). Without this strong verb, the passage would not communicate the action or the character's emotion nearly as effectively. For example, if the narrator used the weaker verb "moved," we readers wouldn't be able to envision his action or make inferences about how he was feeling at the time. When I read Ellison's original passage, I picture the narrator moving quickly and forcefully toward the yellow coin and get a strong sense of the urgency the passage suggests he feels. Without this strong verb, I wouldn't have such a clear and emotionally connected experience.

While the domain-specific language discussed in this section varies based on particular genres, topics, and ideas, it all achieves the goal of ensuring that readers have clear understandings of the information they encounter and that they are able to comprehend texts in the ways the authors of those pieces intend. In the next section, we'll take an in-depth look inside a twelfth-grade class and examine how those students apply their knowledge of domain-specific language and consider its importance.

A Classroom Snapshot

My twelfth graders are obsessed with the Broadway musical *Hamilton*, so it doesn't surprise me when one of the students talks about it before class; what does surprise me, though, is that a student thoughtfully connects the language in the play to the recent conversations we've been having about domain-specific vocabulary: "I was listening to *Hamilton* last night," the student explains, "and I kept noticing strong verbs and specific nouns! I noticed a strong verb really early in the first song and then just kept noticing more and more as I kept listening! There were specific nouns about things in the government and strong verbs that really showed how people did different things."

"That's fantastic!" I exclaim. "It's incredibly cool that you're noticing examples of these grammatical concepts in out-of-school scenarios, like listening to *Hamilton*! Today, we're going to do something similar in class: we're going to work in groups to identify examples of strong verbs and specific nouns in books of your choice."

Class begins, and I introduce the activity to the rest of the students, explaining that they'll work together in small groups to find a strong verb or specific noun in a book they select, replace it with a weaker verb or a more general noun, and comment on why the strong verb or specific noun is important to the effectiveness of the original piece. "This activity is a great way for you to practice identifying these grammatical concepts and to think about why these concepts really make a difference in the quality of a piece of writing. As I mentioned, one of the tasks I'll ask you to complete in this activity is replacing the strong verb or specific noun with a weaker or more general version. You might ask, 'Why would you make something sound worse?' The reason is to really emphasize how important the specific language in the text is to the work's effectiveness. If a sentence uses the specific noun 'dictionary,' and I replace it with the general noun 'book,' it's easy to see how the new version is far less concrete and informative than the original one."

I give each group a copy of the chart depicted in Figure 7.3 and explain it: "This chart is what you and your group members will fill out while you complete the activity. Once you select a book to use, you'll find a sentence that uses a specific noun or strong verb, identify an example of one of those concepts, rewrite the sentence with the specific noun or

Figure 7.3 Graphic Organizer for Student Analysis of Specific Nouns and Strong Verbs

Original Passage	Specific Noun or Strong Verb You Identified	Sentence Rewritten with Specific Noun or Strong Verb Replaced	Why the Specific Noun or Strong Verb Is Important to the Original Passage

strong verb you identified replaced by a more general version, and analyze why that specific noun or strong verb is important to the effectiveness of the passage." (A reproducible version of this chart that you can use in your classes is available in Appendix B.)

"Before I ask you to select a book and get started on this activity," I tell the students, "I'm going to show you an example. I chose to use Shakespeare's play *Macbeth* (1997) for the activity. A line that stood out to me is Lady Macbeth's statement 'I laid their daggers ready' (2.2.11). I thought this line was a good choice for this activity because of its use of the specific noun 'daggers,' so I'll write 'I laid their daggers ready' in the first column on the chart and 'daggers' in the second column. I think a general noun replacement for 'daggers' could be 'weapons,' so I'll write 'I laid their weapons ready' in the third column. The fourth and final column on this chart asks me to consider why the specific noun 'daggers' is important to the effectiveness of the original sentence. For this, I'm going to write 'The word "daggers" is important because it clearly communicates the type of weapons Lady Macbeth is discussing. Without it, we would not have the specific knowledge of the situation that we currently do.' When you work with your group members to complete this activity, make sure you think carefully about why the specific noun or strong verb you select is important to the effectiveness of the sentence. As you work, I'll check in with each group and see what you're noticing."

The students get started on the activity: some select books from the classroom library, others use books they're using for independent reading, and one group picks a text the class read earlier in the year. I move around the classroom, listening to the group's conversations and answering a few questions. After some time has passed, I sit down with a group that appears to be finishing up:

"How's it going, you all?"

"We just finished!" a student cheerfully replies. "Plus, we just use one of my favorite books!" She holds up the novel *Prep* by Curtis Sittenfeld (2005).

"Great," I respond. "I love your excitement! What did you find?"

Another student in the group answers, "We picked out a sentence where Lee, the main character, is talking about a yearbook photo she saw: 'The final section, after the seniors' pages, contained photos of graduation: the senior girls in white dresses, the boys in white pants and navy blazers and boaters'" (p. 21).

"That's a good sentence for this activity," I observe. "What specific noun or strong verb did you identify?"

"We picked out the specific noun 'boaters,'" explains a group member. "It tells the kind of shoes the boys wear wearing. We said that without this specific noun, the sentence would say, 'The final section, after the seniors' pages, contained photos of graduation: the senior girls in white dresses, the boys in white pants and navy blazers and shoes.'"

"Awesome!" I exclaim. "I love how you identified that specific noun and replaced it with a much more general version. The final column on the chart asks you to think about why the specific noun in the original passage is important to its effectiveness. How did you all respond there?"

"We said that the specific noun 'boaters' is important for a couple of reasons," replies another group member. "First of all, it makes the sentence a lot more informative, so you get a lot more specific information when you read it. We thought it was also important because of how it gives off a kind of tone or vibe about the school. This book's about a girl going to a fancy boarding school, and the noun 'boaters' gives information about the school being fancy. The boys don't just wear any kind of shoes. They wear this one fancy kind. It sends a message about the school."

I commend the group on this thoughtful analysis: "That's such a wonderful insight! I'm so impressed by your thoughts about the importance of this specific noun. You're absolutely right that a specific noun like the one you identified can not only give readers specific information, but also use that information to send a message about certain attributes. Awesome work!"

I continue to move around the classroom, thrilled by the specific nouns and strong verbs groups have identified and the students' thoughtful analyses of the importance of these concepts to the excerpts they've identified. I'm also very pleased by the wide range of texts groups have identified, ranging from contemporary fiction (like *Prep*) to canonical literature (one group uses Henry James' *Washington Square*) to nonfiction (another group uses a sports book called *Big Data Baseball* by Travis Sawchik). Once I've checked in with each group, I'm very pleased with the whole class's understanding of specific nouns and strong verbs and how these concepts play important roles in the concrete and effective writing across topics and genres.

Instructional Recommendations

In this section, I discuss a step-by-step instructional process to use when helping students understand the impact of strong verbs and specific nouns and use these concepts to make their writing as clear and effective as possible. I recommend utilizing five instructional steps to achieve these goals: 1) Show students examples of strong verbs and specific nouns used in a variety of published texts; 2) Talk with students about why those strong verbs and specific nouns are important to the texts in which they appear; 3) Have students work together to identify and analyze specific nouns and strong verbs; 4) Ask students to apply the concepts of specific nouns and strong verbs to their own writings; and 5) Help students reflect on how these concepts impact their works. These recommendations focus on helping students develop deep understandings of strong verbs and specific nouns and apply those understandings. With this in mind, I recommend using the information in Figures 7.1 and 7.2 to make sure students understand the essential attributes of these concepts before beginning this instructional process.

1. Show students examples of strong verbs and specific nouns used in a variety of published texts.

This initial step is important to helping students understand the wide-ranging impact of specific nouns and strong verbs: by showing your students how these concepts appear in a wide range of published works, you convey to them that these grammatical choices are tools that all authors use to maximize the quality of their work. Recall that the Common Core Standards call for students to understand how to use domain-specific language in the kinds of writings students will see and use in their college experiences and career: presenting students with examples of specific nouns and strong verbs from a variety of genres enhances the likelihood that they'll see examples that will align with the kinds of writing they'll encounter in the future.

For instance, earlier in this chapter I discussed examples from Ellison's *Invisible Man* and Bryson's *A Short History of Nearly Everything*; these are excerpts I've shared with my students to help them see the many uses of specific nouns and strong verbs. When presenting these examples to my students, I explained to them that I wanted them to see the many ways these concepts are used in writing: "These two books—*Invisible Man* and *A Short History of Nearly Everything*—are very different texts about very different topics, but they both use specific nouns and strong verbs. This goes to show that specific nouns and strong verbs are really widely used grammatical concepts that you'll see in all kinds of writing. You'll see them in the pieces we read in English class, but you'll also see them in reading you do in other subjects and even in the things you'll read for your future careers." In addition to the excerpts from these texts, I've also shown students examples of specific nouns and strong verbs from articles about technology, politics, and sports. I highly recommend bringing in examples from writing about topics your students are especially interested in to show them relevant examples of concrete and domain-specific language!

2.   Talk with students about why those strong verbs and specific nouns are important to the texts in which they appear.

Once you've shown your students examples of specific nouns and strong verbs in a variety of published texts, I recommend talking with them about why those concrete terms are important to the effectiveness of their texts. I like to do this by taking a specific noun or strong verb from a published excerpt, replacing it with more a more general one, and then discussing the differences between the examples with the students. When sharing these original and revised examples with my students, I've found it useful to create graphic organizers that clearly juxtapose the two versions of the text. I project these organizers to the front of the room using the document camera and talk with the students about how the original and revised versions are different, focusing primarily on what specific and concrete information the original excerpts provide and how the revised texts differ. Figure 7.4 contains the selections from *Invisible Man* and *A Short History of Nearly Everything* discussed earlier in this chapter, juxtaposed with how they look with the specific nouns and strong verbs replaced with less-concrete language. (A blank, reproducible version of this graphic organizer is available in Appendix B.)

When discussing original and revised examples with your students, I recommend beginning by thinking aloud about your insights about the first excerpts you share, highlighting why the original version is stronger than the revised one. Then, once students have heard you think aloud and learned the example, you can ask them to take more of an active role in the analyses, inviting them to comment on what makes an original excerpt with specific language stronger than a revised version containing general statements.

Figure 7.4 Comparison of Original and Revised Excerpts

Original Excerpts from Published Texts	Revised Excerpts with Specific Language Replaced with General Versions
"A few astronomers continue to think there may yet be a Planet X out there—a real whopper, perhaps as much as ten times the size of Jupiter, but so far out as to be invisible to us" (Bryson, 2003, p. 29).	A few **people** continue to think there may yet be a Planet X out there—a real whopper, perhaps as much as ten times the size of Jupiter, but so far out as to be invisible to us.
"He lay there, moaning on the asphalt…" (Ellison, 1947, p. 5).	He lay there, moaning on the **ground**…
"In 1795 a selection of bones made their way to Paris, where they were examined by the rising star of paleontology, the youthful and aristocratic Georges Cuvier" (Bryson, 2003, p. 105).	In 1795 a selection of bones made their way to Paris, where they were **seen** by the rising star of paleontology, the youthful and aristocratic Georges Cuvier.
"I **lunged** for a yellow coin lying on the blue design of the carpet…" (Ellison, 1947, p.27).	I **moved** for a yellow coin lying on the blue design of the carpet…

3. Have students work together to identify and analyze specific nouns and strong verbs.

Now that you and your students have discussed why specific nouns and strong verbs are important to effective writing, you can give them more ownership by asking them to work in groups to select excerpts from published texts, identify strong verbs or specific nouns in those excerpts, replace them with more general language, and analyze the importance of the specific noun or strong verb they identified. This small-group identification and analysis (an example of which is described in this chapter's classroom snapshot) provides students with a structured way to apply their knowledge of the importance of specific language. When preparing students to engage in this activity, I like to notify them of the combination of structure and freedom they have: "When you work on this activity with your group members, you'll have a lot of choice, like the book you use, the excerpt you identify, and the specific language you select," I recently told my students, "but you'll also have a lot of structure and support. You have a graphic organizer to use that will help you structure your thinking, and I'll be here moving around the room and will be happy to answer any questions you have."

Before asking your students to complete this analysis, I recommend modeling an example of how you'd complete the activity, as I did in the classroom snapshot with a selection from *Macbeth*. Once you've provided the students with this model and are confident in their understandings, you can ask the students to work together to complete the information on the graphic organizer. (In the example described in the classroom snapshot, I asked the students to use a book of their choosing for the activity. Depending on your preferences and your resources, you can either ask students to choose their own text for the activity or use a book they are studying as a class; either option can work well.) As the student groups work the activity, I like to check in with them and inquire about their progress.

A group of students in the class discussed in the classroom snapshot used the book *Big Data Baseball* (Sawchik, 2015), which describes a Major League Baseball team's strategies for winning games. The group identified the strong verb "snagged" in the sentence "Walker snagged the ball and threw it to first for the out" (p. 102) and replaced it with "caught" in its revised version. A group member then concluded the analysis by commenting on the importance of "snagged" to the original text: "It's important because it tells you exactly how Walker caught the ball. When you snag a ball, you catch it quickly. It's kind of a hard play—you need fast reflexes. The strong verb the author uses shows that. If he had just said 'Walker caught the ball,' the sentence wouldn't be as informative." This thoughtful analysis clearly conveys the importance of the strong verb "snagged" and its impact on the effectiveness of the original passage.

4. Ask students to apply the concepts of specific nouns and strong verbs to their own writings.

When preparing students for this fourth step, which gives them the opportunity to apply their knowledge of these concepts to their own writing, I like to refer to the idea that using specific language carries a level of responsibility: "Specific nouns and strong verbs are really useful grammatical concepts because they allow you as a writer to express your ideas clearly and directly, but there's also responsibility that goes with them: they require you to know the meanings of the words you're using very well. For example, if you're talking about a computer and decide to use a specific noun, make sure the specific noun you're using aligns with what you want to say. If you say, 'We bought a new laptop,' make sure 'laptop' actually represents the kind of thing you're trying to describe."

I tell the students to apply these concepts to their works in two ways: I ask them to first read anything they've already done on the pieces they're creating, looking for any general nouns and weak verbs and replacing them with specific nouns and strong verbs. I tell them that once they're done doing that, then they should keep the concepts of specific nouns and strong verbs in mind as they continue to write. While the students write, I like to hold one-on-one conferences with them, in which I check in on their progress applying these concepts and provide any support they need. During these conferences, I ask students to identify some specific nouns and strong verbs they've used in their writing; this helps me assess their understandings of the concepts and allows me to see how well they're incorporating specific nouns and strong verbs in their writing. I recently spoke with a student who explained that he used the specific noun "sequoia" in his essay about Yosemite National Park to clearly refer to a specific type of tree he saw there that especially stood out to him. Once you've met with your students about their uses of specific language, you can move to the next step of this instructional process: reflecting on the impact of the strong verbs and specific nouns they used.

5. Help students reflect on how these concepts impact their works.

This final step is designed to enhance students' metacognitive awareness of the importance of specific nouns and strong verbs to their works. To help students think carefully about the impact of these concepts on their writing, I like to ask them three related questions: 1) What is an especially important specific noun or strong verb you included in your writing?; 2) How do you feel that specific noun or strong verb enhanced the effectiveness of your work?; and 3) How do you think the quality of your work would be lessened if you didn't use that specific noun or strong verb and used general language instead? I've found that these questions are effective because they ask students to identify an example of specific language they believe is important and carefully consider the effect of that language on the quality of the work.

The student who wrote about Yosemite National Park commented on the impact of the specific noun "sequoia" by saying, "Using 'sequoia' definitely enhanced the effectiveness of my essay because it tells readers exactly what kind of tree I'm talking about. It makes my essay really specific and communicates information really clearly." He then explained that his work wouldn't have been as strong if he hadn't used this specific noun: "If I couldn't use 'sequoia,' the essay wouldn't be as good. My writing sounds a lot better if I say 'sequoia' instead of 'tree.' 'Tree' is really general, but 'sequoia' is specific and shows what kind of tree I'm talking about."

Final Thoughts on Using Domain-Specific Words and Phrases

◆ The term "domain-specific words and phrases" refers to concrete and precise language that authors use to clearly and concretely express ideas and communicate information.

◆ The Common Core Language Standards emphasize the importance of domain-specific words and phrases: Standard L.11–12.6 calls for students to understand and use this concept "at the college and career readiness level" (Core Standards, 2010).

◆ The grammatical concepts of strong verbs and specific nouns allow students to communicate in concrete and specific ways that are relevant to the domains and topics they'll encounter and the genres in which they'll need to write.

  ◆ Specific nouns clearly and directly communicate particular people, places, things, or ideas. General nouns, on the other hand, refer to people, places, things, or ideas in broad and nonspecific ways.

  ◆ Strong verbs indicate the exact ways particular actions are performed. Weak verbs, on the other hand, are vague and don't clearly communicate the way actions are done.

◆ The use of domain-specific language—which can be achieved by incorporating specific nouns and strong verbs—is essential to effective writing because it allows authors and their readers to have the same understandings of key information.

  ◆ Specific nouns are important tools for effective writing because they allow for readers and writers to have shared understandings of the same people, places, things, and ideas.

  ◆ Strong verbs are important to effective writing because they communicate how actions are performed and provide insights into the feelings and moods surrounding those actions.

◆ When teaching students about the use of specific nouns and strong verbs in effective writing:

  ◆ Show students examples of strong verbs and specific nouns used in a variety of published texts.

  ◆ Talk with students about why those strong verbs and specific nouns are important to the texts in which they appear.

  ◆ Have students work together to identify and analyze specific nouns and strong verbs.

  ◆ Ask students to apply the concepts of specific nouns and strong verbs to their own writings.

  ◆ Help students reflect on how these concepts impact their works.

Section **3**

Putting It Together

8

Assessment Strategies

Throughout this book, we've been examining grammatical concepts as tools for effective writing: strategies that published authors use to enhance the effectiveness of their works and that our students can implement to make their writings as strong as possible. How, then, should we assess our students' understandings of the importance of grammatical concepts to effective writing? This question seems straightforward, but it's actually quite complex: we know that assessment and instruction should align (Bratcher and Ryan, 2004), but how can we purposefully and carefully assess our students' knowledge of grammatical tools? I've worked with a number of teachers whose fallback assessment form is to include a section for "grammar" on a writing assignment's rubric, but that often evaluates whether or not students make grammatical errors, not whether they can use grammatical concepts as tools for effective writing. In this chapter, I'll share with you two assessment practices—and corresponding rubrics—that can help you purposefully and carefully evaluate students' understandings of grammatical concepts as tools that writers use to make their works as strong as possible.

Assessment Practice One: Grammar-Focused Literary Analysis

In this assessment practice, students conduct close readings of literary texts, focusing on how the author of the selected text uses a grammatical concept to maximize the effectiveness of his or her work. When preparing students to do this, I tell them that they can either select one book-length text to analyze or choose a number of shorter works (such as poems, short stories, or essays) by the same author. For example, a student might analyze how William Faulkner uses relative clauses in the novel *The Sound and the Fury*, or how Langston Hughes uses strong verbs in several poems. I explain to students that the objective of the assignment is for them to look carefully at the text or texts they're analyzing and think about how the author uses a particular grammatical concept as a tool to enhance the effectiveness of the piece.

In a conversation with a group of students about this assignment, I emphasized its connection to the instruction I'd delivered: "When you write this paper, you'll be doing the same kind of analysis we've done in class when we've talked about examples of certain grammatical concepts in literature and why those concepts are important to effective writing. Remember when we talked about relative clauses and discussed the importance of the relative clause 'dripping with snow and water' to a passage from *Wuthering Heights*? That's the same kind of work you're going to do on this paper. Look for a grammatical concept in a published text that you think is especially important, like one that adds important detail, clarity, and information. Then, when you write the paper, bring in specific examples of the grammatical concept you choose and discuss its impact on the test, just like we've done in our class discussions."

Figure 8.1 depicts the rubric I use when evaluating my students' work on this assignment. (A reproducible version of this rubric can be found in Appendix B.)

Figure 8.1 Rubric for Grammar-Focused Literary Analysis

Criteria	Evaluation Questions	Possible Points	Your Score
Identification of grammatical concepts	Does the paper's author clearly and accurately identify examples of the grammatical concept on which the paper is focused?	5	
Analysis of grammatical concepts	Does the paper's author provide detailed and thoughtful analyses of the importance of the identified concept to the effectiveness of the published text? Is it clear that the paper's author understands how the identified concept enhances the published text?	5	

Total score:

Comments:

When using this rubric with your classes, I encourage you to adapt and add to it in any way you see fit; for example, some teachers like to evaluate on other writing traits than the attributes listed, such as organization and voice. This rubric captures the key components of this assignment's instructional objectives, but can certainly be expanded to meet your specific needs. I tell my students that the recommended length for the paper is around four pages.

Assessment Practice Two: Student-Writing Analysis

This assessment practice connects to another aspect of the grammar instruction described in this book: the strategic application of grammatical concepts to students' own writings and the corresponding analysis. For this assessment, students write two documents: a piece of original writing in any genre and an analysis of how a particular grammatical concept is especially important to that piece of writing. For example, one student turned in a historical fiction short story set in the Civil War and a corresponding analysis of how the prepositional phrases he used in the story are important to its effectiveness. Another student wrote an argument essay on the benefits of the school day starting at a later time and an analysis of the significance of the concept of connotation to the quality of her essay.

Like with the first assessment form, I identify the connections between this assignment and my instruction when explaining it to students, highlighting how the work they'll do mirrors the way they applied grammatical concepts to their own works and reflected on the importance of those concepts. "Every time we discussed a grammatical concept," I recently reminded my students, "I eventually asked you to use that concept in your writing and analyze how it made a difference in your work. That's exactly what you're going to do on this assignment: write a piece in any genre that uses one of the grammatical concepts we've discussed and then write a reflection of how that piece uses the concept and why the concept on which you're focusing is important to the piece."

I tell my students that the length of the piece that uses the grammatical concept is flexible and dependent somewhat on genre: a short story, for example, will be longer than a poem and probably even longer than several poems. I emphasize, though, that their writing will need to be long and detailed enough to contain several examples of the concept they'll discuss in the accompanying analysis. I recommend that students' analyses of their uses of specific grammatical concepts are approximately two pages long. It's important to note that, when evaluating students' performance on this task, I assess the quality of their analysis, not the piece of writing they're analyzing. For instance, when a student turned in the previously-mentioned short story set during the Civil War and analysis of the prepositional phrases used in the story, I only graded the student's work on the analysis. I do, however, make it clear to students that they can't complete the assignment if they don't turn in both their writing sample and their analysis. Figure 8.2 contains the rubric I use when evaluating students' work on this assignment. (A reproducible version of this rubric is also available in Appendix B.)

You'll notice that this rubric is almost identical to the one used for the previous assessment, except that the words "published text" in the first rubric are replaced by "author's writing sample" in this one. I point out these similarities and slight differences to my students, calling their attention to the fact that they're analyzing the significance of grammatical concepts to effective writing in both assignments, even though some of the assignment components differ: "You're doing some different things in these assignments, but the big idea behind each one is the same: think carefully and metacognitively about how and why key grammatical concepts like the one's we've discussed are important to effective writing. Whether you're looking at a published book by an author you enjoy or an example of your own work, the main idea is to consider how grammatical concepts are tools that authors use purposefully and carefully to enhance their works."

Figure 8.2 Rubric for Grammar-Focused Analysis of Students' Own Writing

Criteria	Evaluation Questions	Possible Points	Your Score
Identification of grammatical concepts	Does the paper's author clearly and accurately identify examples of the grammatical concept on which the paper is focused?	5	
Analysis of grammatical concepts	Does the paper's author provide detailed and thoughtful analyses of the importance of the identified concept to the effectiveness of the author's writing sample? Is it clear that the paper's author understands how the identified concept enhances the author's writing sample?	5	

Total score:

Comments:

Notes on Implementing These Assessments

When I share these assessment strategies with teachers, people sometimes ask about the best ways to implement them, such as how frequently they should be used and whether both assessment forms should be used at the same time or separately. I like to give both assignments once the students and I have talked about a number of grammatical concepts so that they have a great deal of choice and flexibility in the concepts they choose. (I've tried asking students to focus on a particular grammatical concept for these assignments, but I've found that the students do better work when given more flexibility.) In terms of a timeframe for the assessments, I like to first ask students to analyze the importance of a grammatical concept to a published text or group of texts. Once I've helped the students create these essays, graded them, and given feedback to the students, I introduce the next assessment, in which students turn in a piece of their writing and an analysis of the importance of a certain grammatical concept to that piece. It's been my experience that this sequence helps students do even better work on the second assessment than they did on the first because they can learn from the feedback I give them on the earlier assignments. I don't require that students use the same or different concepts for the two assignments: I tell them that they're welcome to pick a grammatical concept of their choosing, but, for the sake of the quality of their analyses, it needs to be a concept that is purposefully and frequently used in the original text. These instructions emphasize to students that it's important to look at grammatical concepts as tools that authors choose to enhance their works and suggest the different choices authors make as they construct their works.

Final Thoughts on These Assessment Strategies

- Since it's important to align assessment and instruction, the best way to evaluate students' understandings of the grammatical concepts discussed in this book is with assessment practices that reflect the instruction described in the book.
- Both assessment practices described in this chapter extend from the instructional practices in the preceding chapters and are designed to evaluate students' understandings of grammatical concepts as tools for effective writing.
    - In the first assessment, students conduct close readings of literary texts, focusing on how the author of the selected text uses a grammatical concept to maximize the effectiveness of his or her work.

- In the second assessment, students write two documents: a piece of original writing in any genre and an analysis of how a particular grammatical concept is especially important to that piece of writing.
- I recommend asking them to complete the second assignment after you've evaluated their first one so that they can learn from the feedback they received.

9

Final Thoughts and Tips for Classroom Practice

I recently communicated with a high school English teacher who told me that she was particularly interested in grammar instruction because it was the main thing the twelfth graders she teaches told me they didn't learn enough of in school. "That's a little surprising," I said to myself. "Students wanted to learn more grammar!" The more I thought about the information the teacher shared, though, the more sense it made to me: being in twelfth grade, the students knew enough about writing and language to know that grammar was important, but hadn't learned enough to feel like they mastered the topic. After all, if students don't receive very much grammar instruction, or learn it in limited ways through worksheets, they're not going to feel comfortable with it.

The goal of this book is to provide high school English teachers with a resource that will facilitate effective grammar instruction, the kind of instruction that helps students understand what key grammatical concepts are, why they're important to effective writing, how the students can use the concepts in their own works, and why the concepts can make their works even better. In this chapter, I share six recommendations for putting the ideas, resources, and practices into action:

- ◆ Explain the fundamental components of a grammatical concept.
- ◆ Present published examples of the grammatical concept to students.
- ◆ Talk with students about why the grammatical concept is important to the published example in which it appears.
- ◆ Have students work together in small groups to analyze the importance of the grammatical concept.

◆ Ask students to apply the grammatical concept to their own works.

◆ Help students reflect on how the grammatical concept enhances their writing.

We'll explore each of these recommendations in detail in this chapter.

Recommendation 1: Explain the Fundamental Components of a Grammatical Concept

Before students think metacognitively about the impact of a grammatical concept, they need to understand what it is! The rest of the recommendations discussed in this chapter focus on helping students analyze aspects of grammar and apply those ideas to their writing, but it's important that students have a foundational understanding of the features and attributes of a particular concept. When beginning a discussion on participial phrases with my ninth graders, I explained, "We're going to talk a lot about how and why authors use participial phrases to make their works really strong, but we're going to begin by talking about what this concept is, including how to identify and create it. Once we're comfortable with that, we'll move to the next steps of this process." To help your students understand the fundamental components of the grammatical concepts I present in this book, I recommend using the information found at the beginning of each chapter under the heading "What Is It?", especially the charts that contain examples and explanations of the concepts. For example, when introducing the features and attributes of participial phrases to ninth graders, I used Figure 1.2 to give the students an overview of the concept.

Recommendation 2: Present Published Examples of the Grammatical Concept to Students

This second instructional practice is the next step in students developing deep and metacognitive understandings of grammatical concepts: now that the students are familiar with the fundamental features of a concept, they can enhance their awareness of its use by seeing authentic examples of how it's integrated into published writing. As I've previously mentioned in this book, I often compare examining published examples of grammatical concepts with seeing animals in their natural habitats: just as a researcher studying cheetahs would learn a lot more about these animals by watching them in nature than in a zoo, a student of writing would learn a lot more about subordinate clauses by seeing how they're used in a published text than by looking at examples on a worksheet. When showing your students how grammatical concepts look when used authentically in published texts, I recommend using the book's Annotated Bibliography: this resource lists all the published examples that are featured in this book as exemplars of particular grammatical concepts, as well as information about the specific concept featured in the example and the corresponding Common Core Language Standard. For instance, if you want to show your students published excerpts containing subordinate clauses, you can look in the Annotated Bibliography for examples of this concept. One such excerpt you'll find is the statement "If you wish to inflict a heartless and malignant punishment upon a young person, pledge him to keep a journal a year" (p. 42) from Mark Twain's *The Innocents Abroad* (1869), which begins with the subordinate clause "If you wish to inflict a heartless and malignant punishment upon a young person."

Recommendation 3: Talk with Students about Why the Grammatical Concept Is Important to the Published Example in Which It Appears

Once students have seen published examples of a grammatical concept and have developed an understanding of how the concept looks in the context of authentic writing, it's time to take the discussion to a deeper level by talking with the students about why that concept is important to example in which it appears. I've found that the best way to facilitate these discussions is to show students "before" and "after" examples of the concept's use by presenting them with examples of how a published text looks with the grammatical concept and how it looks without it. For example, if you're talking with your students about the importance of relative clauses, you could show them an example of a published sentence with a relative clause and a revised version of that sentence with the relative clause removed, and then lead a conversation with them about what kind of information the relative clause adds and why that information is important. I recommend displaying both versions of the sentence in the front of the room to give students a clear representation of the differences between them.

When I talked with my students about the importance of the relative clause "where winter slept" to the sentence "Stay away from the maze where winter slept" (p. 123) in Ray Bradbury's novel *Something Wicked This Way Comes* (1962), I displayed the original text juxtaposed with a revised version that did not contain the relative clause. After highlighting these differences, I talked with the students about what the original version conveyed to us that the revised version did not, focusing on the idea that a relative clause, like every other grammatical concept, is a tool that authors purposefully use to enhance the quality of their works. "The relative clause 'where winter slept' describes the maze and adds to the eerie mood of the sentence," I explained to my students. "The sentence would still make sense on a basic level without it, but it wouldn't have the same impact that it currently does if Bradbury chose not to use this relative clause."

Recommendation 4: Have Students Work Together in Small Groups to Analyze the Importance of the Grammatical Concept

This next instructional recommendation releases more responsibility to the students, asking them to work in groups to identify a published example of the grammatical concept they're studying and analyze its importance. There are two ways to organize the students' selections of published examples: they can select a text of their own choosing, drawing from books in the classroom and school libraries as well any other works they have with them, or you can assign a specific text for them to use, such as one your class has recently studied. There are pros and cons to each approach—students selecting their own texts can enhance engagement, while the class using a common book provides more structure and allows all students to have a common point of reference. I recommend balancing these possibilities by asking students to use a text they've previously read for some activities and select works of their choice for some others. For example, when talking with my ninth graders about prepositional, participial, and absolute phrases, I asked them to select a book of their choice and identify an example from that text. However, when working with them on relative and subordinate clauses, I asked them to select an example of one of these concepts from *Romeo and Juliet*, which they had recently finished reading. Each classroom snapshot in this book contains an example of me helping students as they work on one of these activities. I suggest using these descriptions and the corresponding graphic organizers provided in these classroom snapshots (and available in reproducible form in Appendix B) to help you guide your students' analyses.

Recommendation 5: Ask Students to Apply the Grammatical Concept to Their Own Works

I love this step of the instructional process because I really enjoy seeing students use a particular grammatical concept we've been studying in their own writings. I tell students that this is the time when they really get to take ownership of their learning: "This part of the process is all about your writing," I recently told a group of students, "and that makes it really exciting. You'll get to use what we've been talking about to make your writing even better." Before students get started applying a concept to their works, I tell them that there are different ways authors can do this. I suggest that they first reread what they've already written with a particular grammatical concept in mind, looking for places where they can revise the existing work to incorporate that concept. For example, students could look for places to revise weaker verbs by replacing them with stronger ones or for sentences that could be enhanced with the descriptive information relative clauses provide. After students look for text to revise, they can apply the focal concept as they continue to write. When students do this, I caution them that they should use grammatical concepts purposefully and strategically. For example, I don't want them to use relative clauses simply for the sake of doing so; instead, I want them to use that concept when doing so would make the piece as effective as possible.

While students write, I suggest holding one-on-one conferences with them that focus on how the students are doing with integrating particular concepts into their works. In these conferences, I like to ask students to show me examples of how they've incorporated the grammatical concept on which they're focusing into their pieces. If a student is working on adding prepositional phrases to a short story, I'll ask him or her to show me a passage where he or she incorporated this concept into the story. These conferences provide a great opportunity for informal assessment: based on how well a student has used a grammatical concept, I can gain information about the student's level of understanding and if I need to reteach him or her any aspects of that concept.

Recommendation 6: Help Students Reflect on How the Grammatical Concept Enhances Their Writing

While it would be possible to conclude this instructional process at the conclusion of the preceding suggestion, doing so would deprive students of an important benefit: the chance to think metacognitively about how a grammatical concept has enhanced the effectiveness of their works. Asking students to reflect on how using a certain concept improved their writing helps them see the concept as a tool that they can use purposefully and strategically to make their writing as strong as possible. I recommended helping students think about the impact of these instructional practices on their works by asking them to respond to a series of reflection questions that address how using a certain concept made an impact on the piece the student created. While the specifics of these questions will vary somewhat based on the concept, the main components remain the same: I like to ask each student how one or more examples of a grammatical concept made her or his work as strong as possible and how the piece would be different if she or he didn't use that concept. In this book, each chapter describing a specific grammatical concept includes possible reflection questions to ask your students after they apply that concept to their works.

Final Thoughts on The Common Core Grammar Toolkit

Recall the vignette at the beginning of this book, in which I described my experience talking with high school English teachers about the best practices of grammar instruction: during a discussion of combining literature and grammar instruction, I explained, "There's no need to resort to grammar workbooks and out-of-context exercises when you have so many excellent examples of published texts that can guide your grammar instruction." I see *The Common Core Grammar Toolkit* as a resource that helps high school English teachers put effective, literature-focused grammar instruction into practice. As you're now aware, this book contains many examples of grammatical concepts found in literary texts and describes instructional practices to use when helping your students understand these concepts, comprehend their importance, and apply them to their own writings. When you teach grammar in the ways this book describes, you're not doing it alone: you're doing it with the support of Twain, Shakespeare, Hemingway, and countless others whose works are featured in this book as examples of effective writing.

Section 4

Resources

References

Achebe, C. (1st published 1959; edition published 1994). *Things Fall Apart.* New York, NY: Anchor Books.

Anderson, S. (1st published 1919; edition published 1947). *Winesburg, Ohio.* Mattituck, NY: Aeonian Press.

Beah, I. (2007). *A Long Way Gone: Memoirs of a Boy Soldier.* New York, NY: Farrar, Straus, and Giroux.

Bellow, S. (1958). *Henderson the Rain King.* New York, NY: Penguin.

Berger, B. (2016). How humanities degrees cultivate marketable business skills. *Entrepreneur.* Retrieved from: www.entrepreneur.com/article/277828.

Bradbury, R. (1962). *Something Wicked This Way Comes.* New York, NY: HarperCollins.

Bratcher, S., and Ryan, L. (2004). *Evaluating Children's Writing: A Handbook of Grading Choices for Classroom Teachers* (2nd ed.). Mahwah, NJ: Lawrence Erlbaum Assoc.

Brontë, E. (1st published 1847; edition published 1995). *Wuthering Heights.* New York, NY: Penguin Classics.

Bryson, B. (2003). *A Short History of Nearly Everything.* New York, NY: Broadway Books.

Clark, U. (2010). Grammar in the curriculum for English: What's next? *Changing English: Studies in Culture and Education, 17* (2), 189–200.

Common Core State Standards Initiative (2010). Common Core State Standards for English Language Arts. Retrieved from: www.corestandards.org.

Crichton, M. (1990). *Jurassic Park.* New York, NY: Ballentine Books.

Dickens, C. (1st published 1861; edition published 2012). *Great Expectations.* New York, NY: Puffin Books.

Eggers, D. (2009). *Zeitoun.* New York, NY: Vintage Books.

Ellis, J.J. (1996). *American Sphinx: The Character of Thomas Jefferson.* New York, NY: Vintage Books.

Ellison, R. (1st published 1947; edition published 1995). *Invisible Man.* New York, NY: Vintage International.

Faulker, W. (1st published 1929; edition published 1990). *The Sound and the Fury.* New York, NY: Random House.

Fitzgerald, F.S. (1925). *The Great Gatsby.* New York, NY: Charles Scribner's Sons.

Flavell, J.H. (1979). Metacognition and cognitive monitoring: A new area of cognitive–developmental inquiry. *American Psychologist, 34*(10), 906.

Fletcher, R., and Portalupi, J. (2001). *Writing Workshop: The Essential Guide.* Portsmouth, NH: Heinemann.

Gaines, E.J. (1993). *A Lesson Before Dying.* New York, NY: Vintage Contemporaries.

Hardy, T. (1st published 1891; edition published 2008). *Tess of the D'Urbervilles.* New York, NY: Penguin Classics.

Hemingway, E. (1940). *For Whom the Bell Tolls.* New York, NY: Scribner.

James, H. (1st published 1880; edition published 2013). *Washington Square.* New York, NY: Signet Classics.

Killgallon, D., and Killgallon, J. (2010). *Grammar for College Writing: A Sentence Composing Approach.* Portsmouth, NH: Heinemann.

Kolln, M. and Funk, R. (2012). *Understanding English Grammar* (9th ed.). New York, NY: Pearson.

Kolln, M., and Hancock, C. (2005). The story of English grammar in United States schools. *English Teaching: Practice & Critique, 4* (3), 11–31.

Lahiri, J. (2003). *The Namesake.* New York, NY: Mariner Books.

Melville, H. (1st published 1851; edition published 1992). *Moby Dick.* New York, NY: The Modern Library.

Morrison, T. (1977). *Song of Solomon.* New York, NY: Alfred A. Knopf.

Myers, W.D. (1988). *Fallen Angels.* New York, NY: Scholastic.

Orwell, G. (1946). *Animal Farm.* New York, NY: Harcourt Brace and Company.

Robb, L. (2001). *Grammar Lessons and Strategies that Strengthen Students' Writing.* New York, NY: Scholastic.

Ruday, S. (2013). *The Common Core Grammar Toolkit: Using Mentor Texts to Teach the Language Standards in Grades 3–5.* New York, NY: Routledge Eye on Education.

Salinger, J.D. (1951). *The Catcher in the Rye.* Boston, MA: Little, Brown, and Company.

Sawchik, T. (2015). *Big Data Baseball.* New York, NY: Flatiron Books.

Shakespeare, W. (Edition published 1982). *Romeo and Juliet.* R. Gill (Ed.). Oxford: Oxford University Press.

Shakespeare, W. (Edition published 1997). *Macbeth.* Cambridge: Cambridge University Press.

Sittenfeld, C. (2005). *Prep.* New York, NY: Random House.

Thoreau, H.D. (1st published 1854; edition published 2006). *Walden.* New Haven, CT: Yale University Press.

Troia, G.A., and Olinghouse, N.G. (2013). The Common Core State Standards and evidence-based educational practices: The case of writing. *School Psychology Review, 42* (3), 343–357.

Twain, M. (1st published 1869; edition published 2003). *The Innocents Abroad.* Mineola, NY: Dover Publications.

Twain, M. (1st published 1883; edition published 1986). *Life on the Mississippi.* New York, NY: Penguin.

Warren, R.P. (1946). *All the King's Men.* New York, NY: Harcourt Brace and Company.

Weaver, C. (1998). Teaching grammar in the context of writing. In C. Weaver (Ed.), *Lessons to Share on Teaching Grammar in Context* (pp. 18–38). Portsmouth, NH: Boyton/Cook.

Wiesel, E. (1960). *Night.* New York, NY: Bantam Books.

Woolf, V. (1st published 1925; edition published 2005). *Mrs. Dalloway.* Harcourt Brace and Company.

Appendix A
Annotated Bibliography

This annotated bibliography contains the following information: (1) the titles and authors of the literary works that I describe in this book as exemplars of particular grammatical concepts; (2) a key grammatical concept found in each work; (3) the Common Core Language Standard connected with that concept; (4) an excerpt from that work, found earlier in this book, that demonstrates exactly how the author uses that grammatical concept; and (5) information on the chapter of *The Common Core Grammar Toolkit* in which the concept is discussed (in case you want to refer back to the text for more information on a concept).

The annotated bibliography is designed to make this book as user-friendly as possible. It is organized alphabetically by author's last name and each entry includes important details designed to help you use literature to teach these grammatical concepts.

Achebe, C. (1st published 1959; edition published 1994). *Things Fall Apart.* New York, NY: Anchor Books.
Title: *Things Fall Apart*
Author: Chinua Achebe
Grammatical Concept: Connotation and denotation
Related Common Core Standard: L.11–12.5.B
Excerpts that Demonstrate Concept:

"As a young man of eighteen he had brought honor to his village…" (p. 4).
   "There was authority in her bearing and she looked every inch the ruler of the womenfolk in a large and prosperous family" (p. 20).

Discussed in Chapter: 6

Anderson, S. (1st published 1919; edition published 1947). *Winesburg, Ohio.* Mattituck, NY: Aeonian Press.
Title: *Winesburg, Ohio*
Author: Sherwood Anderson
Grammatical Concept: Connotation and Denotation
Related Common Core Standard: L.11–12.5.B
Excerpt that Demonstrates Concept:

"Enoch Robinson sprang to his feet and ran to the window that looked down into the deserted main street of Winesburg" (p. 177).

Discussed in Chapter: 6

Beah, I. (2007). *A Long Way Gone: Memoirs of a Boy Soldier.* New York, NY: Farrar, Straus, and Giroux.
Title: *A Long Way Gone: Memoirs of a Boy Soldier*
Author: Ishmael Beah
Grammatical Concept: Euphemism
Related Common Core Standard: L.9–10.5.A
Excerpt that Demonstrates Concept:

"For a few minutes I tried to image what it felt like for Gasemu when his fingers vibrated to let the last air out of his body" (p. 99).

Discussed in Chapter: 4

Bellow, S. (1958). *Henderson the Rain King.* New York, NY: Penguin.
Title: *Henderson the Rain King*
Author: Saul Bellow
Grammatical Concept: Participial phrase
Related Common Core Standard: L.9–10.1.B
Excerpt that Demonstrates Concept:

"…sitting above the clouds, I felt like an airborne seed" (p. 42).

Discussed in Chapter: 1

Bradbury, R. (1962). *Something Wicked This Way Comes.* New York, NY: HarperCollins.
Title: *Something Wicked This Way Comes*
Author: Ray Bradbury
Grammatical Concept: Relative clause
Related Common Core Standard: L.9–10.1.B
Excerpts that Demonstrate Concept:

"Stay away from the maze where winter slept" (p. 123).
    "And in his eyes were the lost bits and fitful pieces of a man named Fury who had sold lightning rods how many days, how many years ago in the long, the easy, the safe and wondrous time before this fright was born" (p. 169).

Discussed in Chapter: 2

Brontë, E. (1st published 1847; edition published 1995). *Wuthering Heights.* New York, NY: Penguin Classics.
Title: *Wuthering Heights*
Author: Emily Brontë
Grammatical Concept: Participial phrase
Related Common Core Standard: L.9–10.1.B
Excerpts that Demonstrate Concept:

"The intruder was Mrs. Heathcliff—she certainly seemed in no laughing predicament: her hair streamed on her shoulders, dripping with snow and water..." (p. 172).
 "A letter, edged with black, announced the day of my master's return" (p. 199).

Discussed in Chapter: 1

Another Grammatical Concept Featured in this Text: Euphemism
Related Common Core Standard: L.9–10.5.A
Excerpts that Demonstrate Concept:

"He evidently wished no repetition of my intrusion" (p. 6).

"...she turned her vocal artillery against the younger scoundrel" (p. 14).

Discussed in Chapter: 4

Bryson, B. (2003). *A Short History of Nearly Everything.* New York, NY: Broadway Books.
Title: *A Short History of Nearly Everything*
Author: Bill Bryson
Grammatical Concept: Domain-specific words and phrases
Related Common Core Standard: L.11–12.6
Excerpts that Demonstrate Concept:

"A few astronomers continue to think there may yet be a Planet X out there—a real whopper, perhaps as much as ten times the size of Jupiter, but so far out as to be invisible to us" (p. 29).
 "In 1795 a selection of bones made their way to Paris, where they were examined by the rising star of paleontology, the youthful and aristocratic Georges Cuvier" (p. 105).

Discussed in Chapter: 7

Crichton, M. (1990). *Jurassic Park.* New York, NY: Ballentine Books.
Title: *Jurassic Park*
Author: Michael Crichton
Grammatical Concept: Absolute phrase
Related Common Core Standard: L.9–10.1.B
Excerpt that Demonstrates Concept:

"Tim Murphy lay in the Land Cruiser, his cheek pressed against the car door handle" (p. 204).

Discussed in Chapter: 1

Dickens, C. (1st published 1861; edition published 2012). *Great Expectations.* New York, NY: Puffin Books.
Title: *Great Expectations*
Author: Charles Dickens
Grammatical Concept: Relative clause
Related Common Core Standard: L.9–10.1.B
Excerpt that Demonstrates Concept:

"An elderly woman, whom I had seen before as one of the servants who lived in the supplementary house across the back court-yard, opened the gate" (p. 397).

Discussed in Chapter: Introduction

Eggers, D. (2009). *Zeitoun.* New York, NY: Vintage Books.
Title: *Zeitoun*
Author: Dave Eggers
Grammatical Concept: Connotation and Denotation
Related Common Core Standard: L.11–12.5.B
Excerpt that Demonstrates Concept:

"Other workers were just young men: irresponsible and living for today" (p. 19).

Discussed in Chapter: 6

Ellis, J.J. (1996). *American Sphinx: The Character of Thomas Jefferson.* New York, NY: Vintage Books.
Title: *American Sphinx: The Character of Thomas Jefferson.*
Author: Joseph J. Ellis

Grammatical Concept: Semicolon use
Related Common Core Standard: L.9–10.2.A
Excerpt that Demonstrates Concept:

"All the seats on the Senate floor were filled, and the gallery was crowded to capacity" (p. 205). (When revised to include a semicolon, this sentence reads, "All the seats on the Senate floor were filled; the gallery was crowded to capacity.")

Discussed in Chapter: 3

Ellison, R. (1st published 1947; edition published 1995). *Invisible Man.* New York, NY: Vintage International.
Title: *Invisible Man*
Author: Ralph Ellison
Grammatical Concept: Domain-specific words and phrases
Related Common Core Standard: L.11–12.6
Excerpts that Demonstrate Concept:

"He lay there, moaning on the asphalt…" (p. 5).
"I lunged for a yellow coin lying on the blue design of the carpet…" (p. 27).

Discussed in Chapter: 7

Fitzgerald, F.S. (1925). *The Great Gatsby.* New York, NY: Charles Scribner's Sons.
Title: *The Great Gatsby*
Author: F. Scott Fitzgerald
Grammatical Concept: Participial phrase
Related Common Core Standard: L.9–10.1.B
Excerpt that Demonstrates Concept:

"Flushed with his impassioned gibberish he saw himself standing alone on the last barrier of civilization" (p. 137).

Discussed in Chapter: Introduction

Gaines, E. J. (1993). *A Lesson Before Dying.* New York, NY: Vintage Contemporaries.
Title: *A Lesson Before Dying*
Author: Ernest J. Gaines

Grammatical Concept: Semicolon use
Related Common Core Standard: L.9–10.2.A
Excerpt that Demonstrates Concept:

"I didn't want to think about that cell uptown; I didn't even want to think about Miss Emma and the lies I had to tell her" (p. 90).

Discussed in Chapter: 3

Hardy, T. (1st published 1891; edition published 2008). *Tess of the D'Urbervilles.* New York, NY: Penguin Classics.
Title: *Tess of the D'Urbervilles*
Author: Thomas Hardy
Grammatical Concept: Vary syntax for effect
Related Common Core Standard: L.11–12.3.A
Excerpts that Demonstrate Concept:

Multiple-verb sentence: "Mrs. Durbeyfield, having quickly walked hitherward after parting from Tess, opened the front door, crossed the downstairs room, which was in deep gloom, and then unfastened the stair-door like one whose fingers knew the tricks of the latches well" (p. 26).
    Multiple-verb sentence: "They entered upon the turf, and, impelled by an irresistible force, slackened their speed, stood still, turned, and waited beside the stone" (p. 397).
    Inverted-verb sentence: "Among these on-lookers were three young men of a superior class, carrying small knapsacks strapped to their shoulders, and stout sticks in their hands" (p. 16).

Discussed in Chapter: 5

Hemingway, E. (1940). *For Whom the Bell Tolls.* New York, NY: Scribner.
Title: *For Whom the Bell Tolls*
Author: Ernest Hemingway
Grammatical Concept: Vary syntax for effect
Related Common Core Standard: L.11–12.3.A
Excerpts that Demonstrate Concept:

Single-verb sentence: "I will carry the pack" (p. 12).
    Multiple-verb sentence: "He climbed down and took the bucket and helped her up the last boulder" (p. 323).
    Inverted-verb sentence: "On her face there was still a shadow of the expression the mention of the blinding had put there" (p. 223).

Discussed in Chapter: 5

Lahiri, J. (2003). *The Namesake*. New York, NY: Mariner Books.
Title: *The Namesake*
Author: Jhumpa Lahiri
Grammatical Concept: Semicolon use
Related Common Core Standard: L.9–10.2.A
Excerpts that Demonstrate Concept:

"The train guard's portable phone would not work; it was only after the guard ran nearly five kilometers from the site of the accident, to Ghatshila, that he was able to transmit the first message for help" (p. 17).
   "The lights are soothingly dim, and there is only one other bed next to hers, empty for the time being" (p. 22). (When revised to include a semicolon, this sentence reads "The lights are soothingly dim; there is only one other bed next to hers, empty for the time being.")

Discussed in Chapter: 3

Melville, H. (1st published 1851; edition published 1992). *Moby Dick*. New York, NY: The Modern Library.
Title: *Moby Dick.*
Author: Herman Melville
Grammatical Concept: Connotation and denotation
Related Common Core Standard: L.11–12.5.B
Excerpts that Demonstrates Concept:

"Well, then, however the old sea-captains may order me about…" (p. 5).
   "But the side ladder was not the only strange feature of the place, borrowed from the chaplain's former sea-farings" (p. 56).

Discussed in Chapter: 6

Morrison, T. (1977). *Song of Solomon*. New York, NY: Alfred A. Knopf.
Title: *Song of Solomon*
Author: Toni Morrison
Grammatical Concept: Connotation and denotation
Related Common Core Standard: L.11–12.5.B
Excerpt that Demonstrates Concept:
"Everyone knew the girls had spent hour after hour tracing, cutting, and stitching the costly velvet, and that Gerhardt's Department Store would be quick to reject any that were soiled" (p. 5).

Discussed in Chapter: 6

Myers, W.D. (1988). *Fallen Angels.* New York, NY: Scholastic.
Title: *Fallen Angels*
Author: Walter Dean Myers
Grammatical Concept: Absolute phrase
Related Common Core Standard: L.9–10.1.B
Excerpt that Demonstrates Concept:

"Suddenly it picked up speed, wheels squealing, lurching from one side of the narrow street to the other" (p. 87).

Discussed in Chapter: 1

Orwell, G. (1946). *Animal Farm.* New York, NY: Harcourt Brace and Company.
Title: *Animal Farm*
Author: George Orwell
Grammatical Concept: Prepositional phrase
Related Common Core Standard: L.9–10.1.B
Excerpts that Demonstrate Concept:

"For the next two days Boxer remained in his stall" (p. 82).
   "No one stirred in the farmhouse before noon on the following day…" (p. 86).

Discussed in Chapter: 1

Salinger, J.D. (1951). *The Catcher in the Rye.* Boston, MA: Little, Brown, and Company.
Title: *The Catcher in the Rye*
Author: J.D. Salinger
Grammatical Concept: Hyperbole
Related Common Core Standard: L.9–10.5.A
Excerpts that Demonstrate Concept:

"…my parents would have about two hemorrhages apiece if I told anything pretty personal about them" (p. 1).
   "She has about five thousand notebooks. You never saw a kid with so many notebooks" (p. 177).

Discussed in Chapter: 4

Sawchik, T. (2015). *Big Data Baseball.* New York, NY: Flatiron Books
Title: *Big Data Baseball*
Author: Travis Sawchik

Grammatical Concept: Domain-specific words and phrases
Related Common Core Standard: L.11–12.6
Excerpt that Demonstrates Concept:

"Walker snagged the ball and threw it to first for the out" (p. 102).

Discussed in Chapter: 7

Shakespeare, W. (Edition published 1982). *Romeo and Juliet.* R. Gill (Ed.). Oxford: Oxford University Press.
Title: *Romeo and Juliet*
Author: William Shakespeare
A Grammatical Concept Featured in this Text: Subordinate clause
Related Common Core Standard: L.9–10.1.B
Excerpts that Demonstrate Concept:

"If I may trust the flattering truth of sleep, / My dreams presage some joyful news at hand" (5.1.1–2).
  "If you ever disturb our streets again, / Your lives shall pay the forfeit of the peace" (1.1.94–95).
Another Grammatical Concept Featured in this Text: Relative clause
Related Common Core Standard: L.9–10.1.B
Excerpt that Demonstrates Concept:

"By my count, I was your mother much upon these years that you are a maid" (1.3.71–73).

Discussed in Chapter: 2

Another Grammatical Concept Featured in this Text: Oxymoron
Related Common Core Standard: L.9–10.5.A
Excerpt that Demonstrates Concept:
"O heavy lightness, serious vanity" (1.1.168).

Discussed in Chapter: 4

Shakespeare, W. (Edition published 1997). *Macbeth.* Cambridge: Cambridge University Press.
Title: *Macbeth*
Author: William Shakespeare
Grammatical Concept: Domain-specific words and phrases
Related Common Core Standard: L.11–12.6
Excerpt that Demonstrates Concept:

"I laid their daggers ready" (2.2.11).

Discussed in Chapter: 7

Sittenfeld, C. (2005). *Prep*. New York, NY: Random House.
Title: *Prep*
Author: Curtis Sittenfeld
Grammatical Concept: Domain-specific words and phrases
Related Common Core Standard: L.11–12.6
Excerpt that Demonstrates Concept:

"The final section, after the seniors' pages, contained photos of graduation: the senior girls in white dresses, the boys in white pants and navy blazers and boaters" (p. 21).

Discussed in Chapter: 7

Thoreau, H.D. (1st published 1854; edition published 2006). *Walden*. New Haven, CT: Yale University Press.
Title: *Walden*
Author: Henry David Thoreau
Grammatical Concept: Prepositional phrase
Related Common Core Standard: L.9–10.1.B
Excerpt that Demonstrates Concept:

"The mass of men lead lives of quiet desperation" (p. 7).

Discussed in Chapter: 1

Twain, M. (1st published 1869; edition published 2003). *The Innocents Abroad*. Mineola, NY: Dover Publications.
Title: *The Innocents Abroad*
Author: Mark Twain
Grammatical Concept: Subordinate clause
Related Common Core Standard: L.9–10.1.B
Excerpt that Demonstrates Concept:

"If you wish to inflict a heartless and malignant punishment upon a young person, pledge him to keep a journal a year" (p. 42).

Discussed in Chapter: Introduction

Twain, M. (1st published 1883; edition published 1986). *Life on the Mississippi*. New York, NY: Penguin.
Title: *Life on the Mississippi*
Author: Mark Twain
Grammatical Concept: Subordinate clause
Related Common Core Standard: L.9–10.1.B
Excerpts that Demonstrate Concept:

"If he were talking about a trifling letter he had received seven years before, he was pretty sure to deliver you the entire screed from memory" (p. 118).

"If the boat was known to make her best speed when drawing five and a half feet forward and five feet aft, she was carefully loaded to that exact figure—she wouldn't enter a dose of homeopathic pills on her manifest after that" (p. 140).

Discussed in Chapter: 2

Warren, R.P. (1946). *All the King's Men*. New York, NY: Harcourt Brace & Company.
Author: Robert Penn Warren
Grammatical Concept: Hyperbole
Related Common Core Standard: L.9–10.5.A
Excerpt that Demonstrates Concept:

"Boy, I'll tell you, I'm going to have a cage of canaries in every room that can sing Italian grand opera and there ain't going to be a nurse that hasn't won a beauty contest at Atlantic City and every bedpan will be eighteen-carat gold…" (p. 139).

Discussed in Chapter: 4

Wiesel, E. (1960). *Night*. New York, NY: Bantam Books.
Title: *Night*
Author: Elie Wiesel
Grammatical Concept: Semicolon use
Related Common Core Standard: L.9–10.2.A
Excerpts that Demonstrate Concept:

"The people's morale was not too bad; we were beginning to get used to the situation" (p. 18).

"Through the windows we could see barbed wire; we realized this must be the camp" (p. 25).

Discussed in Chapter: 3

Woolf, V. (1st published 1925; edition published 2005). *Mrs. Dalloway.*
New York, NY: Harcourt Brace and Company.
Title: *Mrs. Dalloway*
Author: Virginia Woolf
Grammatical Concept: Hyperbole
Related Common Core Standard: L.9–10.5.A
Excerpt that Demonstrates Concept:

"…she was never in the room five minutes without making you feel her superiority, your inferiority…" (p. 11).

Discussed in Chapter: 4

Appendix B
Reproducible Charts and Forms You Can Use in Your Classroom

This appendix contains reproducible versions of key charts and forms featured in this book. It is designed to help you put the ideas in this book into action in your classroom!

Figure 1.4 Phrase Analysis Chart

Book Title and Author	Type of Phrase You Noticed	Excerpt that Contains Phrase	Why the Phrase Is Important to the Text

Figure 2.3 Clause Analysis Template

Passage Containing a Relative or Subordinate Clause	Type of Clause in Passage	Passage Rewritten without the Clause	Why the Clause Is Important to the Original Passage

Figure 2.4 Sentence Juxtaposition Chart: Relative and Subordinate Clauses

Passage Containing a Relative or Subordinate Clause	Why the Clause Is Important to the Original Passage
"And in his eyes were the lost bits and fitful pieces of a man named Fury who had sold lightning rods how many days, how many years ago in the long, the easy, the safe and wondrous time before this fright was born" (Bradbury, 1962, p.169).	"And in his eyes were the lost bits and fitful pieces of a man named Fury."

Figure 3.2 Graphic Organizer for Semicolon Analysis Activity

Book Used	Passage Containing a Semicolon	How the Passage Could be Written without the Semicolon	Why the Semicolon Is Important to the Original Passage

Figure 3.3 Graphic Organizer for Semicolon Revision Activity

Book Used	Original Passage	How the Passage Could Be Revised to Include a Semicolon	How Incorporating a Semicolon Changes the Original Passage

Figure 3.4 Comparisons of Sentences with and without Semicolons

Original Text	Revision One: Revised to Create Separate Sentences	Revision Two: Revised with a Comma and Coordinate Conjunction Instead of a Semicolon
"The people's morale was not too bad; we were beginning to get used to the situation" (Wiesel, 1960, p. 18).	The people's morale was not too bad. We were beginning to get used to the situation.	The people's morale was not too bad, for we were beginning to get used to the situation.
"Through the windows we could see barbed wire; we realized this must be the camp" (Wiesel, 1960, p. 25).	Through the windows we could see barbed wire. We realized this must be the camp.	Through the windows we could see barbed wire, so we realized this must be the camp.

Figure 4.2 Graphic Organizer for Figure of Speech Analysis Activity

Book Used	Figure of Speech You Identified	How It Appears in the Text	Why the Figure of Speech Is Important to the Passage in which It Appears

Figure 5.2 Graphic Organizer for Syntax Analysis Activity

Sentence from the Text	Sentence Type (Single-Verb, Multiple-Verb, or Inverted-Verb)	Why You Think the Author Chose to Use This Sentence Type
1.		
2.		

Figure 6.2 Graphic Organizer for Student Analysis of Connotation and Denotation

Original Excerpt	Word You Chose to Replace	Replacement Word with Similar Denotation but Different Connotation	New Version of Sentence	How the Meaning of the New Sentence Differs from the Original One

Figure 7.3 Graphic Organizer for Student Analysis of Specific Nouns and Strong Verbs

Original Passage	Specific Noun or Strong Verb You Identified	Sentence Rewritten with Specific Noun or Strong Verb Replaced	Why the Specific Noun or Strong Verb Is Important to the Original Passage

Figure 7.4 Comparison of Original and Revised Excerpts

Passage Containing a Relative or Subordinate Clause	Why the Clause Is Important to the Original Passage
"A few astronomers continue to think there may yet be a Planet X out there—a real whopper, perhaps as much as ten times the size of Jupiter, but so far out as to be invisible to us" (Bryson, 2003, p. 29).	A few **people** continue to think there may yet be a Planet X out there—a real whopper, perhaps as much as ten times the size of Jupiter, but so far out as to be invisible to us.
"He lay there, moaning on the asphalt…" (Ellison, 1947, p. 5).	He lay there, moaning on the **ground**…
"In 1795 a selection of bones made their way to Paris, where they were examined by the rising star of paleontology, the youthful and aristocratic Georges Cuvier" (Bryson, 2003, p. 105).	In 1795 a selection of bones made their way to Paris, where they were **seen** by the rising star of paleontology, the youthful and aristocratic Georges Cuvier.
"I **lunged** for a yellow coin lying on the blue design of the carpet…" (Ellison, 1947, p.27).	I **moved** for a yellow coin lying on the blue design of the carpet…

Figure 8.1 Rubric for Grammar-Focused Literary Analysis

Criteria	Evaluation Questions	Possible Points	Your Score
Identification of grammatical concepts	Does the paper's author clearly and accurately identify examples of the grammatical concept on which the paper is focused?	5	
Analysis of grammatical concepts	Does the paper's author provide detailed and thoughtful analyses of the importance of the identified concept to the effectiveness of the published text? Is it clear that the paper's author understands how the identified concept enhances the published text?	5	

Total score:

Comments:

Figure 8.2 Rubric for Grammar-Focused Analysis of Students' Own Writing

Criteria	Evaluation Questions	Possible Points	Your Score
Identification of grammatical concepts	Does the paper's author clearly and accurately identify examples of the grammatical concept on which the paper is focused?	5	
Analysis of grammatical concepts	Does the paper's author provide detailed and thoughtful analyses of the importance of the identified concept to the effectiveness of the author's writing sample? Is it clear that the paper's author understands how the identified concept enhances the author's writing sample?	5	

Total score:

Comments:

Appendix C
A Guide for Book Studies

The Common Core Grammar Toolkit is an excellent book-study text for groups of high school English teachers who are interested in making grammar instruction as relevant, useful, and engaging as possible by connecting grammar and literature. If you are using this text for a book study, I recommend reflecting on key issues in the book at three distinct stages: before reading, during reading, and after reading. The following sections provide key points to consider before examining the text, while you're reading it, and once you've completed it.

Before Reading

Before reading this text, I suggest activating your prior knowledge of this book's central points by considering these key ideas:

- What challenges do you associate with grammar instruction?
- How are grammar and literature instruction similar? How are they different?
- How have you used mentor texts (existing piece of writing used to teach students a particular writing strategy) in your writing instruction?

During Reading

After reading the book's introductory chapter, answer the following questions:

- In the opening vignette, I tell the teachers with whom I'm talking that grammar instruction and literature don't need to be taught as separate entities. What are some benefits that can come from combining grammar and literature instruction?
- In a description of a discussion I had with students about grammar instruction, I explain, "When you think about grammar, I don't want you to just think about identifying mistakes; I want you to think about why authors use certain grammatical concepts and what those concepts add to their writing." Why might it be beneficial to think about more than just identifying mistakes when talking about grammar?

Next, I recommend answering the questions below with your study-group members at the conclusion of each chapter between Chapter 1 and Chapter 7:

◆ What published example discussed in the chapter especially stood out to you as an effective usage of the chapter's grammatical concept?
◆ What did you notice about the students' analyses in the classroom snapshot? What adaptations might you make when asking your students to complete similar analyses?

After that, read Chapter 8 and discuss the following questions with the other members of your book-study group:

◆ What are some challenges you associate with evaluating students' usage of grammatical concepts?
◆ What strikes you as effective about the assessment strategies described in this chapter?
◆ What are some additions or adaptations you'd make to the rubrics discussed in the chapter?

Next, read Chapter 9 and discuss the following with your group members:

◆ How do you feel the steps of the instructional process described in this chapter, when used together, can help you create effective grammar instruction for your students?

After Reading

Now that you've finished *The Common Core Grammar Toolkit*, talk with your book-study group about your responses to these four questions:

◆ How have the ideas in this book changed your perception of grammar instruction?
◆ What are some examples from the annotated bibliography that you think will work especially well with your students?
◆ What are some other works of literature that are particularly interesting to your students and that you can use to show your students effective uses of grammatical concepts?
◆ What are some grammatical concepts with which you feel your students especially need help?
◆ What is one way that you feel this book will immediately impact the way you teach grammar to your high school students?